Dedicated to my wife, Mary

CONTENTS

Front cover by Simon Laurie, Artist

CONTENTS

Front cover by Simon Laurie, Artist

FOREWORD

I got to know Terry Welsh only a little bit, towards the end of his life. He was a friendly, amiable man whose conversation combined inquisitiveness with a type of Glasgow cheeriness. With his passing, though, in 2006, and the publication of this book, I wish I had striven to know him better.

I now discover, having read this delightful memoir about Lambhill and Possil, the place of Terry's upbringing in Glasgow, that he was an acute and exquisite observer of time, place, people and habit.

Lambhill, to the north of Glasgow, might not be well known by many people. It sort of abuts onto open countryside with, on clear days, the Campsie hills to be seen in one direction and Dumgoyne and the distant Trossachs in another. But don't get me wrong: Lambhill was not some rural idyll (though it bordered one). What it was in those days of the 1940s and 1950s was a community of warm, hardworking people whose children, like Terry, saw all of life's challenges amid the miners' cottages and cramped, sometimes stinking tenements of the time.

This book teems with memories of a Glasgow community's love, fun, hardship and, in the case of the infamous Cadder mining disaster, terrible tragedy. There are vulnerable women and proud, hard-drinking men in these pages; local villains; yelling, excited children leaping into the Forth and Clyde canal in drowsy high summer; some dubious women, some deadbeats; inspiring school teachers and much more.

When I first read this book I instinctively jumped on my bike from central Glasgow and cycled out to Lambhill – as it is today – to try to discover the specific terrain as set out by Terry. For instance, I cycled from St. Agnes's Church, still standing today and from where the priest and grief-stricken parishioners ran that dreadful day in 1913, over the fields to the now defunct Cadder pits on the banks of the canal, where death and disaster had struck. I'm not sure why I did this. I guess a part of me wanted to go back into the pages of this vivid book, to go back in time almost.

This story is, for me, a beautiful testimony to a time and place in Glasgow that deserves never to be forgotten. Some of it is just hilarious, too. So in memoriam I say to him, well done Terry Welsh…your voice prevails, you have left us a wonderful gift.

Graham Spiers, June 2013

PREFACE

The local history of the Lambhill and Possil area has interested me for many years. The everyday life of the area has provided me with very many, mostly happy, memories of family, friends, neighbours, places and events. In addition, some material is included from elsewhere when it touched upon the lives of the folk from Lambhill and Possil.

I want to put some of these memories on paper to preserve them before they are forgotten entirely. Maybe the stories, anecdotes and pictures will bring back happy memories to older readers and provide younger readers with information about these districts that so many of us love.

I've been encouraged in this endeavour by a number of people and I would like to express my grateful thanks to the following who gave their time, expertise and advice so readily: Tommy Burns, Eddie Connelly, Helen Donnelly, Jim Donnelly, George Facenna, John Faithfull, George Greig, Michael Kerins, Campbell Loudon, John Mains, Eddie Mignano, Jackie McCambridge, Charles McGarry, Kathleen McInch, Charlie McKenna, Kathleen McKenna, John McLaren, Christine McLean, Jean Ritchie, David Scott, Brian Sharp, Brian B Skillin, Bill Spalding, Bill Taylor.

Terry Welsh, 2005

LAMBHILL

Lochfauld Raws, better known by its nickname 'The Shangie', was a miners' village on the north bank of the canal within a mile east of the Lambhill Bridge, consisting of 26 houses with dry toilets at the rear. Three water pumps at the front were provided for washing and cooking. Villagers filled their buckets in the evening for next day's needs. It is alleged that an old seafaring character passing through the area of Lochfauld during the busy industrial period remarked that it reminded him of Shanghai – and so the Shangie became the adopted name of the village.

The wee red-brick school located behind the Shangie houses was the route to Steven's farm and Nos. 15 and 17 collieries. Soldiers were billeted there during World War Two.

Nan Jackson was the last inhabitant of Lochfauld and lived in the former schoolhouse. She was a familiar lone figure walking along the canal bank. Nan's nephew and I were 16-year-old surface workers at Balmore Coal Mine for a period and frequently cycled the canal route. It was a welcome break to have tea in Nan's after a day's shift at the coalmine.

Many mining communities had their share of characters and the Shangie more than others. Nan's niece told me that when they lived in the Shangie, her mother was always concerned whenever her sons visited the 'Lazy Man's' single-end to play cards. He was a clatty, miserable character who drank tea from a jam jar and used his thumb to spread butter. It was

Terry (left) and a friend at the Shangie

Terry performs some impressive gymnastics

common practice that the men of the mining community would be known by their nicknames e.g. Reddy McBride, Tortol McCallum, Ching Kelly, Puff Ferns, The Dreadful Man, Iron Heart and the much loved Inky, my mother's Uncle John. Old Inky was completely illiterate and signed his name with a cross. He also had a bad speech impediment but was an individual of amazing ingenuity and character, full of fun and mischief. The number of stories and legends about his pranks and sayings could fill volumes.

Inky was down the pit working at a section on his own when a new man was asked to give him some assistance. The new man asked Inky, "Whaaat-will-a-dae-tae-help?" Inky grabbed him by the throat, "Aaaarau-makeha-fool-aa-me?" Inky was gobsmacked to discover that his new partner also had a serious speech impediment.

The legendary Inky Elliott takes a dip in the canal

A Hurl for Nothing

It was an unwritten law that any villagers the worse for drink would be escorted safely along the banks of the canal. Old Inky was returning home and on this particular occasion, sober, but very tired. He came upon some workmen repairing the bridge at Bishopbriggs when he noticed an empty wheelbarrow at the towpath and hearing some young lads nearby arguing about football, he lay down beside the barrow pretending to be drunk. The young men, following the usual practice, decided to take him home. As Inky correctly assumed, he was placed on the barrow and the lads, taking it in turns, wheeled him all the way back to the Shangie. When they arrived at his house he leapt from the barrow, thanking them for the lift home. The mind boggles at the expletives uttered.

John Darroch

It was quite remarkable that the Shangie produced so much sporting talent and so many outstanding characters. John Darroch could be described as the unofficial leader of the community. He always had a keen interest in their welfare. John arrived in Scotland as a youth from Ireland and worked at Cadder, eventually becoming a mining contractor at No.15 colliery. This talented Irishman assisted many people from Ireland to find work and a house in the district. On the odd occasion, young men arriving at the Broomielaw from Ireland would stop individuals on the streets of Glasgow and ask for directions to John Darroch's pit. An exceptional sportsman, he was, for more than 50 years, one of the best clay-pigeon shots in Britain, competing in many international events, and was a well-known, respected individual at all levels of society.

Mr. Darroch's career as an expert clay pigeon shot must have been unique. In 1925, as an old man of 65, he took part in an international shoot at Lambhill where he was representing Ireland against the best shots from Scotland and England. When he died in 1931, the Evening Times published the following article:

Glasgow Sportsman's Death

A Glasgow sportsman who was well known all over Scotland, Mr. John Darroch, The Square, Lambhill, [late of Lochfauld] died in Stobhill Hospital yesterday after a three-month illness. Mr. Darroch, who was 71 years, belonged to Glenarrife, County Antrim but came to this country as a youth. He was a noted rifle shot and represented Ireland for three years in succession, in the International Clay Pigeon Shoot, as well as taking second place in the clay pigeon championship of Britain three times. He won scores of prizes and for some time acted as coach to the West of Scotland Gun Club.

Kenmure Raws

My mother's family lived in Kenmure Raws on the other side of the canal which was built around 1853 and housed miners' families in 12 two apartments. An outside sink was shared by two families with dry toilet provision at both ends of the row. Her father was a miner in Cadder Pit. When she was only eight, her mother died and she stayed with her Uncle John, the legendary Inky Elliott, in a single-end in the Shangie.

My grandfather, Terence Elliott, moved from Kenmure to Crawford St, Lambhill, and reared four sons and two daughters on his own. He continued to work as a miner.

Rather than take the long walk to Lambhill Bridge, villagers crossed to the north side of the canal in an iron punt which had a chain attached and was secured to both sides of the canal.

This self-propelled primitive vessel was in use until 1929 prior to the people being rehoused in Lambhill and Possilpark in the 1930s.

The Valley

Mavis Valley was situated on the north side of the canal between the towpath [canal bank] and Wilderness Plantation. The houses were built in two rows from 1855 onwards. The older houses had six privy middens at the end of the raws. Newer houses had one closet for four houses. Wash day took place outside at the rear of the houses. The miners' raws consisted of 116 houses east of No.17 pit which locals referred to as the 'big pit'; and the huge 'bing' between the Valley and the row of modern houses at the bottom of Cawder Woods was a familiar landmark. A number of Valley children walked along the canal bank to St Agnes's Primary in the late thirties and forties. From the upper levels of the black-and-red buildings in Lambhill, residents could view life in Mavis Valley quite clearly, especially the busy Co-operative at the bottom of the village.

Possil Raw was a single row of miners' houses close to Lambhill. The site was used by swimmers for many years and was known as 'The Pier'. The remains of the landing stage are still visible.

The Cadder Pit Disaster

On the afternoon of Sunday, August 3, 1913, a maintenance shift of 26 miners, which included some young lads, reported for work at No.15 colliery in Cadder, north of Lochfauld on the banks of the canal close to Cawder Woods (often referred to as the Bluebell Woods). It was just another shift. They set out with their pieces, flasks of cold tea or cold water and many with chewing tobacco

Mavis Valley with tenement at top of village

Possil Row miners' houses

to keep the mouth moist in the dry, dusty conditions down below. While the men were at their allocated work stations, a fire started in a bothy at the bottom of the brae and quickly spread throughout the workings. Tragically, before 8pm that evening, only four men of the entire shift remained alive. The others were struck

Crowds at the Cadder pit head

down by the poisonous 'white damp' (carbon monoxide). Three of the miners, Felix O'Neil, Robert Dunbar and Michael Keenan, on the advice of the fireman in charge of the shift, Charles Reilly, hurriedly made their way to the interconnecting road to No.17 when they became aware that smoke and poisonous fumes were penetrating the workings. The three survived. Reilly, the shift deputy, returned to warn some of the other men and lost his own life. He left a widow with seven children.

When the pit-warning whistle was heard, families and relatives, also local miners and officials, made their way to the pit head from every direction.

Father Mullen and his young curate Fr O'Hanlon from St Agnes's were conducting devotions when they heard the emergency sound. They immediately finished the service and hurried along the canal, followed by many of the congregation, up the path at Lochfauld and beyond Steven's farm to the pit head at No.15 colliery. With the confusion and panic of people arriving at the pit head anxious for news of their loved ones, the clergymen, Rev J. Woodside Robertson of Cadder Church and the two priests did their utmost to comfort the people who were in a state of shock, fearful for their men folk trapped below ground. When people realised that rescue operations were being conducted from

No.17 colliery, the large crowd, anxious for news, had to be controlled by the police as they made their way across the fields.

Doctor Miller

W. Dick, leading his party of 10 men on the first rescue attempt from No.17 inter-connecting road, didn't encounter any problems until they reached the door forming the air lock into No.15. When the door was opened the three men at the entrance dropped to the ground struck by carbon monoxide. They fell to the ground clear of the door, which closed itself, and were dragged to safety. They were brought to the surface and treated by Dr Miller who had arrived at the pit head from Bishopbriggs. They eventually recovered.

The officials meeting at the pit head quickly decided that reversing the airflow was their only hope to reach the workings in No.15 and clear the air in the passages for a rescue operation. When the airflow started to operate in reverse, smoke and fumes poured out from the main shaft. The first of many rescue parties, including officials and experienced miners, held little hope of finding anyone alive. Although a second rescue group failed, there were plenty of volunteers to organise another rescue team. It was announced at 10pm that they would descend with some of the men carrying canaries, as a safety measure on such a highly dangerous journey. Everyone was desperate to get to the men underground. At the crowded pit head, Dr Miller was busy with the volunteers badly affected in the rescue attempts, assisted by the devoted and tireless county health visitor, Nurse Winchester. She volunteered to go down the pit if necessary.

Progress was slow and dangerous from No.17 pit due to the narrow roads and steep gradients, with frequent checks to test the air for white damp. They reached the main 'dook brae' at the air crossing and discovered five dead miners close to a dead pony. They were identified as George McMillan, George Harvey, Robert Ramsey, Patrick Duffin and Patrick Darragh.

It was agreed that the men had been dead for a considerable time due to carbon monoxide gas. The young pony driver, 15-year-old Owen McAloon, was found dead with his arms wrapped around the animal's neck. After several rescue attempts, the other members of that tragedy were found, some at their allocated work stations. Michael McDonald was the only survivor. He was found against a wall with his face covered in dirt, hidden by dead ponies. When examined and turned over on his back, the rescue party got the fright of their lives. He started snoring loudly. It was a miracle that he had survived those poisonous conditions.

Fr Mullin requested permission from the pit officials to visit the air crossing to administer the Last Rites to Michael MacDonald. The priest was given a miner's cap and lamp and went down the pit with his escort. Fortunately, after extensive treatment over a long period in hospital, MacDonald recovered from his frightening ordeal.

The names of those who died were, from Mavis Valley: George Davidson; three brothers, Alexander Brown, age 15, William, 17, and John, 19, who all lost their lives in the bloom of their youth.

Two other brothers from the Valley also perished. William and Robert Ramsey had been to Rothesay for two weeks and weren't due back to work till Monday, but presumably returned early as they needed the money.

From Possil: Cuthbert Bell, Bardowie St; George MacMillan, Carbeth St; Thomas Holland, Mansion St.

From Lambhill: James Flynn, Drummond St; George Harvey, Drummond's Land; Owen McAloon, Lambhill Crescent; Hugh McCann, Lochfauld Village; Patrick Duffin, Drummond St; Alexander Dunbar, Lambhill Square; James Flynn, Drummond St; Patrick Regan, Drummond's Lane.

Hugh Anderson lived in Lambhill House (the Castle). He was a lad of 18 and the eldest in a family of five. His father had gone to Australia some months previously and preparations had been made for the family to be reunited in that country. Seventeen-year-old Patrick Darragh was a brusher at the pit, which was a man's job, and had recently married Jean Quinn, a girl aged 16. She was left a widow after only four weeks.

From Jellyhill: Alexander MacMillan, Maryhill; Charles Reilly, Summerston; John Worthington, Blackhill Row.

From Garscube Rd: Charles Armstrong.

It was declared safe to bring all the bodies to the surface at around 3am. Dr Miller went down the pit and was led to the air crossing to examine the dead. He notified the senior officials on the surface that death was due to carbon monoxide gas. One per cent of this deadly gas in the air results in instant death. Nothing could be done about the fire until all the men had been brought to the bottom of No.17. The cage came to the surface with one victim at a time who were placed in the engine room for identification, until all members of that tragic shift had been accounted for. Dr Miller meticulously examined all the dead in the temporary mortuary and wrote his findings which were to prove important in the subsequent fatal accident investigations. After an exhausting 12 hours, he left Cadder Pit with silent gratitude from the whole mining community. This remarkable doctor had shown great stamina and endurance, and by his care and attention he identified with the sufferings of all affected by the disaster. His dedication forged a special bond with the mining community.

Thirty-six-year old Dr James Blakely Miller had came to the area in 1901 as an unmarried doctor and continued to practise medicine in the community for 54 years.

After the examinations were concluded, and the airflow returned to normal, the fire fighters, after an arduous journey from Fife, arrived at the scene at approximately 3am to tackle the fire which was out of control and sweeping through the workings of No.15 colliery.

Interment

Wylie and Lochhead Funeral Directors were instructed by the Carron Company to handle all the arrangements. The large, horse-drawn vans delivered the coffins to the victims' homes. The two smaller coffins of 15-year-olds Alexander Brown and Owen McAloon caused more tearful scenes. Two lads cut off in their youth.

Each family affected was given £10 by Carron as temporary help. United in their grief, the village communities agreed to attend as many of the burials as possible. A service was held in the Mission Hall, Mavis Valley at 1.30pm for Alexander, William and John Brown, William and Robert Ramsey, George Davidson and Alexander McMillan. They are buried in Cadder Cemetery. Rev. William Steven from Possilpark conducted a service in the house of Andrew Dunbar and Hugh Anderson. Both men are buried in Lambhill Cemetery. A funeral service for Cuthbert Bell was held at his home, 61 Bardowie St, Possilpark, and he is buried at Riddrie Park Cemetery. The service for Charles Armstrong took place in his father's house, 48

Cadder Pit procession

Crowds gather for the procession

Rolland St, Maryhill, followed by interment at the Western Necropolis.

Remains of the 11 victims were received into St Agnes's in Balmore Rd the previous evening. A huge crowd was in attendance. The coffins were placed in front of the three altars and draped in black. Charles Reilly was a parishioner of Our Lady of Immaculate Conception, Maryhill, but his family thought it proper that he should lie in St Agnes's with the miners he gave his life for.

The funeral parties of Andrew Dunbar and Hugh Anderson were the first to walk in procession to Lambhill Cemetery. Fr Mullin led hundreds of his parishioners behind the procession to the cemetery.

Requiem mass was offered for the 11 miners of his own parish amidst terrible scenes of anguish. It was estimated that over 3,000 people were in attendance. Offices and factories in the districts of Bishopbriggs, Possilpark and Lambhill closed as a mark of respect for the victims and their families.

Fr Mullen preached: "In the midst of life we are in death." His concluding remarks were that 11 members of his parish had been hale and hearty at church on Sunday morning.

"Their call had been swift and sudden. The sad and terrible calamity that had bereft 11 homes of members of their congregation, as well as a number of other homes, of their nearest and dearest, was in some way like the roll of dead in a battle.

"The death toll at Cadder Pit where the departed brethren had lost their lives was different; they had nothing to fight for, they were engaged in the bowels of the earth earning a livelihood to support their near and dear ones."

The 11 miners of St Agnes's are buried in a mass grave in St Kentigern's Cemetery, Lambhill, situated behind the Western Necropolis.

Far from every miners dwelling in and 'round the Mavis Vale,
Immediately all thoughts of pleasure fled,
When the miners' wives and families had heard the awful tale,
That caused so many salt tears to be shed
And the fire horn blowing.
Set the human stream fast flowing,
to the pit whose clouds of black smoke filled the air.
And all hearts grew sad and sadder,
As they neared the pit at Cadder,
While their hope for those entombed
below had bordered on despair.
But the tide of their emotion swelled into a mountain wave,
And to stay their tears the bravest were unfit.
When they saw the rescue part fine lads born to brave,
Volunteering to descend the smoking pit,
Into Hades they descended,
Little caring though life ended,
If only one man living they restored,
To a poor grief-stricken mother,
To a sister, to a brother,

To a wife, or child, or lass that he adored
Often from such dashing fellows have our foemen backward reeled,
On many a well disputed battleground;
"And scores of do or die men" [pit disasters have revealed],
Amongst the miners always can be found.
But to fear, in time of danger,
Every miner is a stranger,
For, when working to great danger he's exposed;
Thus his usage makes him master
And a hero in disaster,
Where he's always pretty cool and self composed
Handsome Dickson and Young Johnston who so nobly led the way,
By the fumes, became unconscious underground,
But by skilful aid they rallied, and again, without delay,
On the cage with brave companions they were found.
In their bold attempt the second,
Prudence to the party beckoned,
And told them to retire before, as
soon as they intended,
Again they all descended,
And found five together lying with whom life's fight was o'er
But hark! there comes the wagon with eight gallant lads from Fife,
And each equipped with his lifesaving kit,
And down the vale of sorrow those heroes in the strife,
And sent up all dead and living in that pit,
They found together fifteen others,
Two and three of whom were brothers,
And a boy and little pony lying side by side,
And brave Reilly who had perished,
For the mates whose love he cherished,
Whom he nobly tried to save before he died.
Cowdenbeath men, Mavis Vale men,
I would make you men of fame,
If my poor enfeebled pen possessed that power,

But it takes a major poet to immortalise a name,
But may God rich blessings on you shower,
Ah, how like his loving Saviour,
Was that Priest in his behaviour,
Putting on a miner's bonnet and descending to bestow,
The 'last rites' to some poor fellow,
And who made old Satan bellow,
When he whispered words o comfort to
McDonnell down below.
Of the six and twenty miners engaged in Cadder Pit,
At the time the fatal accident occurred,
Only four amongst that number, came out alive from it,
And the rest, alas were piously interred,
Ah, what tears, what signs of grieving,
What prayers, when o'er them heaving,
Was the red earth, and their graves about to close,
Where nothing will encumber,
Their calm and peaceful slumber,
Where kind friends softly laid them to repose.

Wm. Markham Brown

Footnote

After the disaster, No.15 colliery, owned by Carron Company, was abandoned and No.17 became over-manned. Fr Mullen had served in Duntocher and Partick before taking charge at Lambhill in 1905. His traumatic experience caused him much pain and heartache. He departed from Lambhill to St Mary's Pollokshaws in August 1916 and died 18 months later after a prolonged illness, aged only 53.

The preacher at the requiem paid an eloquent tribute to the memory of this remarkable man, recounting his heroism at the Cadder Pit disaster. He went down the pit on two occasions to

St Agnes' plaque

administer to the entombed men, at great personal risk. Fr James Mullen is buried in St Kentigern's Cemetery, Lambhill.

Many local miners didn't attend work the day of his burial in January 1918. A commemorative plaque on the confessional door in St Agnes's Church reads: 'To the memory of the Reverend Father James Mullen, Rector of this Church for 12 years, who died 23rd. Jan. 1918. R.I.P.'

The Annie

The first Shangie miner to come into contact with the crew of 'The Annie' was Robert Jackson. He and his wife were returning home after a visit to the photographers with their new baby. They came upon the small cargo boat drifting out of control close to Lochfauld with the three-man crew drunk and incapable. To the dismay of his wife, as he was wearing his one and only good suit, he immediately gave assistance. The vessel was half-filled with dirty water, and some of the contents were floating about in the canal. After a bit of a struggle it was eventually secured to the canal bank.

A short time after the boat was secured, the crew disappeared, and a few drunk men on their way home retrieved some articles floating in the canal. What they found resulted in the invasion of the deserted boat.

The events of that night of December 26, 1914, were to leave their mark on the people of the village for many years. Nothing was known about where the crew had gone. It was assumed that they had made their way back to their point of departure at Port Dundas, many hours later. They related a story that was incredible to the authorities at the canal basin, that they had been attacked by miners who started to plunder the boat.

Lambhill police were asked to investigate. When the constable arrived at the Shangie on his bike the next morning, he found many men well fortified and some villagers helping themselves to the goods floating in the canal and also in the abandoned boat. Summing up the situation, he returned to Lambhill and reported the matter to Crowhill Rd police station, Bishopbriggs.

Early in the affair, the Shangie men saw a large barrel half submerged in the boat which they salvaged and, by heroic efforts, hauled on to the canal bank and proceeded to roll it into the village. They speculated what it might contain. Ching Kelly pierced the barrel with his miner's pickaxe and placed his finger into the hole to taste the contents; his beaming smile said it all. Whisky! Ching made a proclamation rather than an announcement, which caused much excitement and the spoils had to be shared by all. Villagers appeared with an assortment of containers for their share of the water of life.

A large police force duly arrived at the village and was deployed in and around the little rows of houses. Many of the men were in buoyant spirits and were transported in a wagonette to Bishopbriggs police station.

Although the excitement was at fever pitch, the officer in charge realised that a good number of villagers had slept through the night unaware of what had taken place. As the police continued their search they found many items had been hurriedly concealed on their arrival. On the roof of one house they found a box of currants and a box of fish cutlets, and in another house, a sack full of odd shoes. Many things were found which were not worth hiding. Among them, a large iron pot filled with butter which was confiscated by the police from the house of Agnes O'Brien. It was of little value, but nevertheless was to cause her and her family much suffering and hardship.

During the search, some angry men confronted the police which resulted in them being fined two days later. John Ferns, John Elliott and James Tonner were fined 15 shillings each, or 10 days in prison. Peter Quinn was fined seven shillings and sixpence or five days in the nick.

The police entered the But 'n' Ben of John Elliott – Inky – a man of many talents. The smell of whisky was everywhere. By late morning, after much jollification, Inky was determined to retain his medicine by secreting it under the bed and out of sight in the 'essential utensil'. When the policeman was in the proximity of the precious stuff, Inky reacted with his earned reputation, 'as fly as a jailer'. As only a desperate man would, he slipped a links sausage into the 'essential utensil' just before the representative of the law looked under the bed and withdrew the receptacle, which he hurriedly shoved back under the bed in utter disgust and left the premises, apologising to Inky for the inconvenience. Inky joyfully danced an Irish jig, his treasure intact.

Another incident connected with the *Annie* concerned old Jimmy Cassidy, a miner from Mavis Valley, a short distance from Lochfaulds. Jimmy was a good practising Catholic who walked along the canal bank every Sunday morning, in all kinds of weather, to St Agnes's church in Lambhill. On that particular Sunday, Jimmy was hailed by Ching Kelly and persuaded to cross in the old punt to the Kenmure which resulted in him missing the chapel without any good reason.

He not only missed Mass, but never returned home. His family were obviously concerned. Searching the canal bank they found him quite drunk at the Shangie, singing bawdy songs at the top of his voice. It was fortunate that they found him before he joined the Shangie folk in the wagonette to Bishopbriggs police station.

Excitement was high as people gathered outside Crowhill police station, Bishopbriggs. Many others crossed Cawder golf course to the Shangie. Rumours had grossly exaggerated the whole affair as people were transported to Crowhill Rd in great numbers from the Shangie, to the sympathetic cheers of the curious onlookers.

Amidst all the excitement, some of the older Shangie boys showed a remarkable sense of history and opportunism. When the police operations were in full flow in the early afternoon, boys appeared in the increasing crowds at the Shangie selling a newssheet only a few minutes old entitled 'The Shangie News'. The boys had gathered all the facts about the whole affair, written them down on ordinary sheets of paper and were selling this new journal as fast as they could for a penny a copy. Of all the newspapers which reported the happenings of the *Annie*, the improvised 'Shangie News' was the only one that gave a true report of the events. It is a pity that a copy of it has never been found. Perhaps, somewhere in a household in Glasgow or Bishopbriggs, it exists. Legend and rumour has maintained that on Cawder golf course lies buried very mature whisky in a variety of containers.

The trial took place in Glasgow on June 19, 1915, amidst great excitement. The list of stolen items was read in court as evidence of which a small amount had been recovered, not including the whisky and beer. Eight pounds of butter, 224 pounds of currants, six pounds of raisins, salmon, 17 packets of fish cutlets, 14 pounds of coffee, bottles of beer, one barrel of whisky, a chest of drawers, 22 ladies blouses, two pairs of blankets, one sack with 31 shoes and a large number of small items.

After all the evidence had been heard, Sheriff Thomson said that this was a very serious crime and had no hesitation but to inflict the severest penalty. To a shocked courtroom, he sentenced Thomas Ferns to three months hard labour in Barlinnie Prison and Neil McBride to 60 days. McBride was 18 and supported his widowed mother and the entire family.

Alice Kelly, a mother of two young children, was led to the cells in a state of severe shock when sentenced to 21 days imprisonment. Agnes O'Brien was also sentenced to 21 days in jail. She had four young children at home and was heavily pregnant. Agnes O'Brien's daughter, a wee girl of nine, had to look after the family with the help of neighbours.

Tammy Ferns, a good family man, completed his term in prison with no ill effects. Perhaps being a tough miner and fiercely competitive Junior footballer helped him in the prison environment. He resumed his career at centre-half with Ashfield Juniors and could out-jump the opposition, which was quite remarkable as he was only about 5ft tall.

The severity of the punishment caused much hardship to the individuals and was deemed as a collective shame on the whole miners' village. When Tammy Ferns returned to the Shangie I am sure he was welcomed and celebrated as a hero. Possibly some of the secreted whisky was resurrected for the occasion.

Grandpa and Granny Ferns lived opposite my family in the top landing in the 'Black Building' in Lambhill, and the *Annie* incident was never discussed. We eventually left the building and moved to Milton in 1948.

Life in Lambhill

When you meet people from Lambhill the conversation will inevitably be about days gone by, remembering the families and characters from the Black and Red buildings. Molly Neilson oc-

Agnes O'Brien

cupied a single-end at the back close in 646 Balmore Rd with her husband Walter and their daughter, also called Molly.

Big Molly, as she was named by the locals, was a legend in her lifetime. She was never numbered amongst the church-going population but lives on in the hearts of Lambhill people for her outstanding qualities as a person. In the summer months, she had the window wide open and would be singing like a lintie, settling disputes with the children in the back court while distributing a piece 'n' jam and cool drinks to all and sundry.

Lambhill was a big adventure playground with open country bordered by the canal and lush farmland. Featured in the recreational life of the community was St Agnes's football park with the 'wee lawn' at the canal end, and the red blaes old Lambhill football pitch and converted railway carriage as the pavilion on the far side from the canal. A large grassed area at the bottom of the park was called the 'big lawn'.

Over the back woods was a hilly area situated between the two football fields and divided by a burn. The 'Woods' were great for sledging, and in summer, sliding down the hills on pieces of cardboard. The majority of the tenement residents had a clear view of the back woods and therefore children could be summoned at short notice. The footpath from the Lambhill Bridge, known as the high-bank, merged with the path from Kilfinan St In those long, hot summers children would lie down prostrate and drink from the clear spring water known as the 'springy' beneath the big tree directly behind St Agnes's school. Throughout the school holidays, Molly would organise a picnic to the 'sawny', a small sandy area approximately a mile from the Black Building and a safe distance from the canal for children. These outings were greeted with excited expectation.

About 30 weans assembled in the back court laden with sandwiches and Irn-Bru. Before the safari commenced, she who must be obeyed laid down the ground rules. To be barred from this adventure was serious. Like the Pied Piper, Molly led us on to the bank with the mammies waving frantically and shouting instructions.

We walked along the path to Sandy Munro's wooden house and small holding then beyond the swing over the stinky burn. On the right-hand side, the corn was as 'high as an elephant's eye' in Osborne's field before the fork where the high-bank and low-bank footpaths merged.

The route continued past the pier, a landing stage and former site of Possil miners' row which was popular with swimmers on Sundays. In fact, swimming in the canal was illegal and when the local constable from Lambhill police station cycled along the canal it became a farce. All the swimmers swam to the other side with their clothes held aloft. It was amusing to see dozens of men and boys fleeing from the frustrated, lone policeman bellowing "Ah know yer faces, ah'll get you all the next time!"

We continued along the footpath to the bend in the canal. Although our destination was not yet reached, most of the pieces had already been demolished, supplemented by easily picked brambles, in spite of Molly's remonstrations to keep something for 'efter'. We wearily reached our destination, with Nan Jackson's house the only remaining relic of the famous Shangie miners' houses clearly visible on the opposite side of the canal.

On the odd occasion, Molly would be accompanied by wee Rosie Berrie who was disabled but forever cheerful. She was a very devout person with a lovely smiling disposition and a well-kent face in Lambhill. They both kept a watchful eye on their charges throughout the picnic while knitting endlessly.

When the dreaded announcement was uttered, "It's time to go hame", all shoes and sannys had to be inspected and the site left spick and span before the trek home. Molly eventually flitted from the back-close house to the front of the building.

Her husband, Wattie, was a big cheerful man who also loved children about the house. Wattie came home from the pit one particular day complaining about a sore leg. Being the practical person she was, Molly immediately replied, "Hurry up with yer tea and get a quick wash. Dr Montgomery is still open". The first thing the good doctor said to Wattie was, "Roll up both trouser legs". Poor Molly was fair affronted. Wattie had only washed his sore leg.

School Bully

At the morning interval in St Agnes's Primary I was playing football at the gable-end of the Black Building within the school when my big sister Sadie tearfully told me that the school bully was pestering her. Later, while kneeling to tie my laces for the umpteenth time, I became aware of the big lump of a creature from Possil towering over me. "You wee smout, what are you going to do about it?" he said. Some children formed a circle to view the drama. With Benny Lynch precision I delivered a punch from the ground which landed under his chin. He rose two feet

St Agnes' Primary class

in the air and landed on his back, completely humiliated. My classmates surrounded me as the hero of the day with admiration and friendship, including "Do you want my stump?" (apple core).

Mr. Denver, the janitor, ordered me into his office. He was a much-respected person. Expecting a rebuke and a lecture about fighting, I was surprised when with a beaming smile he gave me a cake and a clap on the back. To be praised by Mr. Denver was special.

At times, help was needed for tattie howking at Osborne's farm, which was back-breaking work. Mrs. Horn, an independent, tough widow from down Lambhill formed a partnership with my mother, who was equally tough from a miner's background, and they were grudgingly assisted by my sister and myself. Thankfully it didn't happen too often!

There was always some form of excitement around Lambhill. Cattle freely grazed at the high bank of the canal in the summer months near Lambhill Bridge and occasionally a cow would topple over into the canal. The farmer would arrive with three pieces of rope for the rescue operation. After the ropes were secured on the animal, the farmer and some local men would pull it up the steep slope to safety.

Rambling clubs were always passing through the area and in need of some refreshment which was provided by wee enterprising Granny Kelly at the red blaes football park. An old worthy remarked that she was so expert at making sandwiches she could spread the contents across the Jamaica Bridge and would have some left over.

Black Building, 652 Balmore Rd

The area which this three-storey building occupied is now just an empty space. The boundary wall around St Agnes's school from

Black Building residents

the gable end with the half-round shiny top has remained intact and the remnants of the iron railings separating the two back courts are in the same position.

Looking at this site in the present day, it's remarkable that in those early days the back court had a wash-house, drying green and midden with ample room for innumerable games.

Back-court concerts were performed the odd time but were held more often in the bigger back greens at the Balmore Rd intermediate housing with Eddy Murphy's Punch and Judy speciality act. Eddy was a natural funny man.

In Our Close

First on the left was the lobby. Charlie Ward and his family stayed in this single-end. He was a nice wee cheery family man who was in the army for the entire war without leave. His wife was a friendly soul and welcomed my family into her single-end when

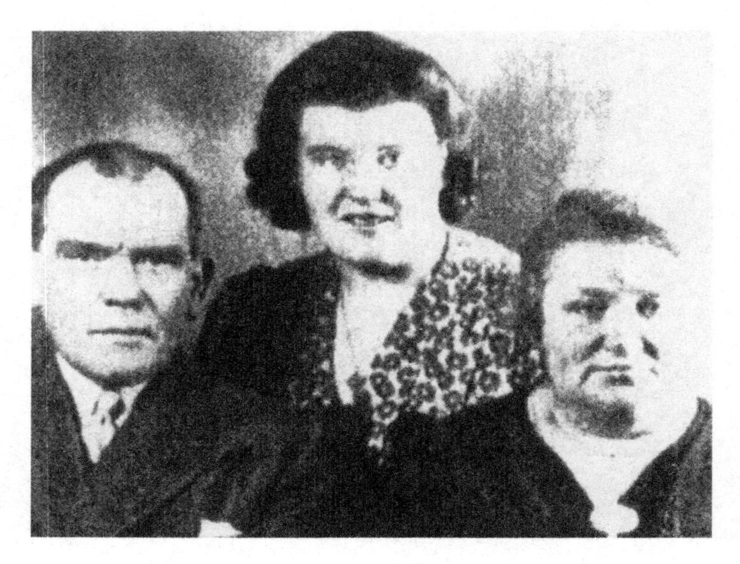

The Ferris family (Black Building)

the blitz was fierce. With two adults and 11 weans, you couldn't swing a cat in that wee room. Also ben the lobby were the Dixons who were a quiet, hard-working family.

When they moved on, the Careys flitted from one up. Kate Carey never married and looked after her father and brothers. They were an adult family who made a fuss of all the children up the close. Dan, John and Matt quite often would take five or six kids and give us a borrie – sitting on the crossbar – on their bikes for a wee hurl along the canal bank. Matt Carey had a cheery personality and was involved with the thriving Boys' Guild football team in partnership with big Dinnie Rogers, a larger-than-life character who wore crepe sole shoes, colourful shirts and bright ties. Dinnie travelled the world from time to time in the construction business. In fact, he was the foreman in the firm responsible for the erection of the Exhibition Tower at Bellahouston Park in 1938.

The Loudon family owned the fruit shop and stayed in the backshop before moving one up alongside Cissy and Bobby

Deary, with Barney Carey and his young family on the opposite side. Bobby Deary was part of Lambhill folklore.

Jim the greyhound, Bobby's faithful companion, would wait patiently for his master's return from the local hostelry or wee Cissy after her working day in Corry's ginger works. Cissy was a great one for the chapel!

Arriving home from school, it wasn't unusual to find a rabbit or a hare lying on the sink board with blood everywhere (courtesy of Bobby). My mother was an expert in preparing these delicious treats.

Barney Carey was a cheery, hardworking coal miner. Quite often on warm sunny days, especially on Sundays, he would grab a big bar of carbolic soap and have a bath in the canal at the 'Pier'. Maybe being entombed below the surface in dangerous and wet conditions, deprived of God's light, coming home with the smell and dirt of the pit, had an effect on miners' personalities because they were a remarkable and resilient breed of people.

When Barney's free ton of coal was dumped on the road near to the close mouth, everyone would lend a hand, fill a bucket and take it up to his door.

Bobby Deary and Charlie McKenna at the Shangie

Miners

Although there was a bunker in the kitchen and also the lobby, it was a mystery as to how he managed to hide all that coal in a wee room and kitchen!

On the second landing lived the Gillespies with their two children. Mr. Gillespie owned a motor bike and sidecar and took great pleasure in taking some children for a wee jaunt, which was a great treat. The Feeney and Rennie families lived on the same landing. Mr. Rennie was an outstanding swimmer in his day. On Sundays, Lambhill men would dive from the wooden bridge watched by people en route to the graveyard or strolling along the canal bank. Johnny Rennie would be poised on top of the bridge railing and would then make a Johnny Weissmuller perfect dive and wouldn't surface for ages. He had a reputation for swimming under water for a longer period than anyone in the district.

The Feeneys were friendly people. Mr. Feeney worked part-time in Mallon's pub with Mr. Marsh from the Red building and big handsome Joe Denver who sadly died a relatively young man. His brother John worked for over 50 years, a lifetime, in the pub, as the owner's right hand man. They were all dressed in smart white shirts and ties and immaculate white aprons worn from the waist and almost reaching to the floor.

The top flat of the building consisted of my mother, father, three brothers and three sisters all crammed into a room and kitchen with, of course, the bed recess in each room. This was a house of happy memories. Our immediate neighbours on the landing were the McGeachy family. Mr. McGeachy lost an arm in World War One but this didn't prevent him riding his bike. He could sit a child on the crossbar without any hesitation. His artificial arm hung in the food cupboard and he used it to tease children for a bit of fun. Tragically, their youngest son Peter died of meningitis aged 10.

The Ferns family were also on the top landing. Tammy Ferns was the aforementioned wee stocky miner who played centre-half with Ashfield. Alice McGeachy and Jeanie Ferns were in the Land Army during World War Two. There was great excitement on our landing when Jeanie was to be married to a soldier in St Agnes's. The great day arrived and the close entrance was packed when she came down the stairs resplendent in white dress and long veil, on the arm of her brother, in soldier's uniform. The bride was

Locals at Wooden Bridge at canal

at the close mouth and the train-bearers were still on the first landing. It was a very windy day and the short walk to the church was a wonderful sight with the veil suspended in the horizontal position unaided.

The Convenience

Twenty-three people shared the stair head toilet on our landing. The draughty interior usually had a broken window and no lighting but plenty of reading material. A kind of 'in-house library'. Swan Vestas matches were in plentiful supply and also big douts (fag ends). Each toilet was identified by a family on their particular landing, a kind of 'toilet supremo'.

Dcary's toilet always had a broken window and served as a general convenience because the door was never locked. It had a permanent puddle of water on the floor and, of course, was bereft of the customary 'lavatory seat'. Probably it served the residents for emergency sittings only.

Rennie's toilet was top of the premier league. This lavvy was state of the art. It was kept in mint condition with wee neat squares of newspaper placed on two protruding screws on the wall and the toilet seat scrubbed almost white. Even the pipe clay line continued in an unbroken line from the landing outside around the edge of the wall and weaved its way around the toilet bowl and back out to the landing. If the opportunity arose on the rare occasion to skip-in before the door was locked, you sat in those hallowed premises absolutely petrified. Every family had a large key which in many instances got mislaid from time to time. The lavatory key had a double purpose. It was also placed down a child's back to stop a continuing nose bleed.

The other close was 646 Balmore Rd, with the Neilsons on the ground floor, as previously mentioned. Jimmy Hart and his two sisters lived one stair up. He was a nice, happy man and a dedicated passkeeper in St Agnes's. Katie and Rose were members of the popular talented choir, renowned throughout the Glasgow Archdiocese. Opposite the Harts were the Ferguson family. Mr. Ferguson was a stocky, cheery man whose great love was his local football team, the very successful Lambhill United. Their home ground was the red blaes pitch at the canal. He was the team trainer and always had the smelling salts and the magic sponge.

Once, a ferocious football game was in progress at the red blaes park when the Gypsy Queen approached the open Lambhill Wooden Bridge. All local children loved to watch this majestic white boat when it passed. Lively music was played from its top deck and passengers would throw coppers to children on the canal bank. On this occasion, Jack McDougal with his brother Charlie, Alfie Ferguson, and myself were anxiously waiting for the ball to be played to one end of the pitch to let us dash across the other end of the park. We eventually made a beeline for the other side and when I was halfway across, the ball was suddenly blootered in my direction. I woke up stretched out on the trainer's table. Mr. Ferguson's salts did the trick assisted by the pungent smell of Sloan's Liniment.

On the second landing were the Miller family. During the Blitz when the old building was shaking, my family were welcomed into the Miller's household until the siren at the police office sounded the all-clear. Wee Harry, Willie and Danny Birt were bachelors on the same landing. Danny was the resident barber and cut hair for a tanner while Willie told jokes. Gerald and Tommy Byrne lived on the top landing.

Gerald is still resident in the district. Petesie McVey also lived on the top level.

The Red Building

These houses had a tiled close, and were grafted on to the Black Building. They are occupied to the present day with the luxury of inside toilets. Mrs. Muir and her husband Guy occupied the house on the top landing and owned the newsagent shop.

Mrs. Muir was a nice, smiling, kindly woman. Her husband was from the showbusiness fraternity and quite often sported a bow tie, even when he accompanied me on the paper round to Osborne's farm and the toffs' houses in the Switchback area. The Muirs were a devoted couple and, in fact, they died within a day of each other. Their top landing neighbours were the large Connelly family. Mrs. Wilkinson who taught in St Agnes's Primary for many years, stayed on the middle landing and had a clear view of the school playground, much to the discomfort of local children. The Marsh and MacIntosh families were the other tenants in the close.

Kilfinan St housed the Gillies family and the Stewarts who had a ferocious dog named 'Help' which hated local weans.

The Earlie family, and Mr. Elliott, a hard-working grave digger, and his wife and son James, lived there also. The Brodie family owned the dairy and were resident on the first floor.

Red and Black Buildings, Lambhill

Auchengillan

In the winter of 1940, I became an enthusiastic member of the 135 Ogilvie Scout troupe which had their headquarters in a big, rambling, haunted mansion situated at Dalhousie St and Buccleuch St in the Garnethill district of Glasgow. The fact that I had to travel from far-flung Lambhill in the depth of winter to dark and sinister Garnethill didn't deter me. After persistent pestering of my poor mother, I was duly fitted with the standard shirt, neckerchief, toggle and lanyard but minus the all important Baden-Powell hat. I was desperate to earn badges, proudly worn by other scouts. Sometime later, after much scrimping and scraping, the dented hat was acquired for 12 and sixpence. To earn the cookery badge required a weekend at Auchengillan scout camp close to Carbeth and providing your own food. Little did I realise the ordeal that lay ahead. With only three weeks until my great adventure, the costly essential rucksack proved to be beyond my mother's means. She had my three brothers and sisters to consider. My father, home on leave from the army, teasingly suggested: "Why not take the big suitcase lying on top of the wardrobe?"

"People would laugh at me going camping with a suitcase," I replied.

However, determined not to miss this great adventure the suitcase was duly removed, dusted and filled with the necessary provisions of porridge oats and an assortment of tins, probably enough to feed the whole troupe. Assisted by the rest of the family, the great weight was pushed and shoved down from the top landing and eventually on to the 22 tram bound for Cowcaddens.

Approximately 70 scouts were assembled at the tram stop all dressed in the full regalia. Kilts, rucksacks, daggers in the sock and well-earned badges were all in view. They were all shocked and dismayed at seeing me with a big leather suitcase. When we

Kenmure Arms (Mallon's); dog and two figures

arrived at the Milngavie tram terminus, I was relegated to the rear for the trek to our destination. The troupe were all cheerfully singing a medley of hiking songs but I was rapidly being left behind as my fellow scouts began to disappear into the distance. My pal Jim Black persistently retreated to share my heavy burden and I arrived exhausted at the campsite half-an-hour after the others. Auchengillan lived up to all my expectations. Singing at a huge bonfire, drinking cocoa and bedding down under canvas.

There were many happy experiences in the Scout movement especially the 'gang shows' held annually in the Theatre Royal. Everyone had a part to play. After months of rehearsals, the big night arrived. My mother, brothers and sisters eagerly waited for my two-minute showbusiness appearance and then the final curtain, with the entire troupe on stage, all proud to be boy scouts.

Learning to Dance

In the early forties, many households were on a diet of Victor Silvester on the wireless. The chairs were placed against the walls in the kitchen and the table was in its usual position in the middle of the room. My mother and sisters were ready for action at the start of the programme. Initially a chair was the partner but soon I graduated to dancin' with my mammy. After a while, you got gallus and danced with your sisters.

Slow, slow, quick-quick-slow. and then the music would stop and Victor would explain everything. Some blokes guided or steered their partners around the dance floor. They couldn't master the rhythm, or were described as having two left feet.

Dancing classes in the red school youth club were open to junior and senior members and Margaret, the dance instructor, was a big smasher. On the odd occasion, when you were asked to be her partner (probably with a big riddy), it was magic. A good many of the senior members would queue up to dance with the teacher. One bloke in particular was great at the tango, especially when he wore his rolled-doon wellies.

Down Lambhill

Craig's Post Office down Lambhill always reeked of paraffin. The McLeans had the fruit shop next door. They eventually acquired Craig's and converted the premises as a combined grocery and post office which was sold after three generations living and trading in the area. Hannah's Cafe next to the post office was always a popular rendezvous on Sunday evenings. It had a toilet on the premises, which was a definite advantage.

They also opened a chip shop. Lambhill folk were spoiled for choice with two cafes within a short distance from each other.

Baird's, the ice-cream cafe at the tram terminus, was popular with local people and visitors from surrounding districts. It was always jam-packed and did a roaring trade with people going to the graveyard or young folk walking the canal bank or strolling out as far as McBrearty's piggery looking for talent. This ritual continued until the demise of the trams.

Baird's also established a chip shop down the wee slope at the rear of the cafe and merged with the two houses occupied by the McAllister family and Mrs. Horn. Saturday and Sunday evenings were exciting with the brass band from the Lambhill

Mission Hall playing to huge crowds at the tram terminus. All those good people would do their stint on the soapbox and preach with great fervour. Before the Cadder housing scheme was created, Lambhill district was in open country and often referred to as the village.

Lambhill House (the Castle) was a well-known landmark which was built in 1788 by the Graham family who lived there until the beginning of the nineteenth century. The Castle was taken over by Glasgow Corporation. I recall several families staying in spacious rooms on the ground floor. I remember visiting

Old Lambhill

my friends the Munro boys there, and I recall the entrance led into a wide hallway. The floor had large, loose flagstones which had to be carefully walked on, as I imagined it would open up to a dark dungeon. For many years the blind flower seller sat against the stone boundary wall with her faithful dog in all weathers before she moved to her pitch outside Hannah's Café.

A friend of mine, Harry Sweeney, was staying with his granny above Baird's and recalls a policeman jumping on to the tram as it slowly left the terminus. A lamplighter was standing on the platform with his brass pole and the cop mistakenly grabbed the wrong pole. Ouch!

Our local lamplighter wore the hat and jacket of his uniform, flannel trousers and white sandshoes. He lit the gas on each landing and then ran like hell to the lamp at the lane leading up to the Switchback. Maybe he was training for the Ibrox Sports.

The Meter Man

When the 'gas man' came to empty the meter he was fascinating to watch. The table in the middle of the floor was cleared as he performed his duties in jig-time, emptying the pennies as we all stood eagerly around the table. He stacked all the pennies in a row and would give my poor mother a stern look of rebuke if he found Irish coins. After his speedy calculations, the rebate was placed on one side and recorded in his book. It seemed so unfair that his share was always bigger than ours. The rest was put into wee pokes and placed into the brown leather bag. He departed with the threat, "If I discover any 'duds' next time, I will have to report the matter to a higher authority". One bloke broke into his meter. When the gas man was due, he replaced some of the pennies stacked in wee neat bundles back into the meter.

Stables at Lambhill

En route into the country, over the old wooden hump-backed bridge, is a large stone structure originally built as stables for trace horses when the canal was a busy waterway. The building was at a later date a facility for wedding functions and social events, known locally as the Hibs' Hall.

Popular dancing was held there regularly. Probably it was the only local community hall in the area for many years. At the Balmore Rd end of the Stables, three families lived in the lower sections of the building which had a small display of flowers at the front with white-painted walls just like country cottages. The Morrow family occupied a two-storey house at the opposite end. At present, this landmark has fallen into disrepair but hopefully there are contingency plans for its restoration.

Lambhill Ironworks

Lambhill Engineering (formerly Allans), which was situated at the tram terminus, was established in 1875 and employed a large workforce many of whom were local or from nearby Possil. From the 1970s, the works were in decline. Before its closure in 1978, the works constructed the new walkway from Renfrew St into the Savoy Centre. The demise of an important engineering establishment was a terrible loss to a district already affected by high unemployment.

Corry's cider and soft drinks factory in Knapdale St, which started trading in 1932, closed its doors in 1977. These premises had been previously used for building small aircraft.

Up Lambhill

The Co-op grocery in Kilfinan St closed at 1pm on Saturdays and, therefore, there was always a buzz about the place as they stocked up for the weekend. The oil and paraffin store next door was self-service and had that wonderful, distinctive smell. It was also exciting to watch the huge blocks of ice being unloaded for the butchers and the drayman transferring large barrels of beer, on straining ropes, down into the cellar of Mallon's pub.

Whilst waiting in the Co-op for their number to be called, two women were discussing their neighbour. "Aye, she got all her teeth oot and an interior grate in the same day."

Mr. Doran's cobblers hut was situated next to the oil and paraffin shed. He worked over his last for hours on end, chatting to local worthies and children were always welcome. Being a regular spectator in the cobblers when he had an attack of the drouth, I was dispatched to Mallon's 'family department' with his special beer can with the handle, and the warning not to taste or spill his tipple. That wonderful smell of leather and the amazing sight of Mr. Doran tossing a handful of nails into his mouth without a break in his conversation is a lasting memory.

A Mallon's outing

Another Mallon's bus outing. Terry's parents (on far right of back row)

A tram passing the Terminus Cafe

At the bottom of Kilfinan St was a large, crumbling stone building which was used for storing building material. In the distant past it had been possibly a fine solid house.

The Coup, John St, 1912

Mr. Welsh, the owner of the Mecca cinema and former Lord Provost of Glasgow, occupied the magnificent red sandstone house at Balmore Rd and Kilfinan St, with its extended garden and stables. When he vacated the property, the house became the manse for Mr. Hogg, the Church of Scotland minister. He was a very gentle man. At a later date, the Baird family (of the Terminus Cafe) lived in this property for a good number of years before departing to the luxurious McConnell's [the shipbuilders] estate, in beautiful Blanefield. The Labour Party were the last occupants of this fine mansion and, at a later date, it was demolished for modern housing. One more landmark erased from old Lambhill.

A boundary road at the back of the stables led to the 'coup' and McNicol's bungalow at the Switchback. Much to the consternation of Lambhill children, whenever there was a wedding in St Agnes's and the ritualistic scramble, the roadside stank claimed some of the proceeds.

From time to time, the 'cleni', with its long suction tube, removed and dumped the muck at the coup beyond the wee wooden huts which were situated parallel with the steep path that led up to Birsay Rd. Like the town crier, someone would shout "Here's the Stanky" which was the signal to descend on the coup to rummage for goodies. On reflection, not a healthy pastime.

Sunday Buskers

Our Sunday ritual very seldom varied, with my mother preparing all the family for 10am Mass. The kitchen window was wide open and on the multi-purpose window sill, the white sandshoes stood freshly whitened. When spotted by the back-court singers they served as a signal for a shaky rendition of 'Bless this House' or the odd verse of 'The Old Rugged Cross' which necessitated an extra penny – sometimes hand delivered or thrown from the window. The performer would dramatically acknowledge as if performing at La Scala Milan Opera House.

Delivering Sunday papers left little time for sartorial fussing to attend the 12pm service. Wearing the old sannies, which always had a hole in the sole of the right foot, warranted emergency action. In those days, the well-dressed congregation in St Agnes's received Holy Communion on their knees at the altar rails, which was embarrassing for yours truly. On the way down to the kneeling position, the left foot was placed behind the punctured sole, therefore the ritual was performed in one effortless movement. Down and up, nae bother! Dignity was retained.

On Sunday morning, Mr. Thorn, the local haulage contractor, would proudly emerge from his stable yard with the handsome, polished buggy (horse and trap) and well-groomed horse. He would travel around Lambhill, kindly picking up children for a wee treat up Balmore Rd, Hillend Rd and then down past the three haunted houses at the plots, turning right at Hannah's Cafe and depositing his charges back at the Black Building. Thorn's horses were left out to graze in the Lambhill back woods after their journeys to and from the busy Speirs Wharf, Buchanan St station and various destinations in and around the city.

Alec the Smithy, opposite the tram terminus, was an important person in the district. If he was assisted at the bellows, to keep the fire at a good level for shoeing the horses, boys were allowed a wee puff. It was fascinating to watch him handling these huge animals. I was convinced they were scared of this wee slip of a man, puffing at his clay pipe and screaming "Stand still ya stupid big eejit!" One particularly massive, fearless horse named Jim had to be stabled at the cooperage off Balmore Rd. He was probably too disruptive to be contained at Thorn's yard. This animal had a real liking for Alec and obeyed his every command. After being groomed and placed in its stall, Jim would bolt the course and head for the Smithy. What a spectacle seeing this wild horse bolting down Balmore Rd beyond Hillend Rd, sparks flying as it careered between the tram rails, much

Illustration of a wild horse

to the consternation of the tram driver, with a full load travelling ahead over the hill and his counterpart coming from the terminus.

There were two brave, popular Lambhill tram drivers, Willie Denholm and big John McInally, who didn't hesitate to resolve the situation. If either was on duty at the time one of them would leap from the driver's cabin and grab the horse around its neck and block the air flow, therefore preventing a possible disaster. They received grateful nods from all the passengers.

The view from our top window was panoramic. It was a wonderful sight to watch the majestic Gypsy Queen pleasure boat glittering white in the sunlight, sailing west from Mavis Valley mining village moving calmly beyond the mountain of pit-bing and heap of discarded waste, a reminder of hard sweat and toil of generations of miners. An attractive row of reddish-brown glazed brick houses with neat gardens lay at the edge of the Bluebell Woods, smoke billowing from their chimneys. They had been upgraded for pit management staff.

Further west was the last house on the north side of the canal, wee Nan Jackson's cottage, the last remaining house of the once thriving Lochfauld community. A red-brick building behind the cottage had been a school for miners' and farm workers' children.

Many characters passed through rural Lambhill and unfortunately were ridiculed by local children. Johnny Hunnercoats (real name John Gilbert) was a harmless big man with a distinctive appearance, wearing two or three coats.

'Peter the Painter' cycled through Lambhill with paint brushes strapped on the back of his bike. Very few people were aware of his skill manufacturing furniture in his house near Blackhill Rd.

The Blitz

When the ARP (Air Raid Precautions) knocked on all the doors in the building and the warning siren from the police station sounded off, every family had to make a hasty retreat to the cold and draughty air-raid shelter in St Agnes's school. There were two shelters situated in the school and the choice was always the one furthest away from the building.

One frightening night, the blitz never ceased. Everyone was terrified, with incendiary bombs falling in high Maryhill resulting in many deaths. One large bomb landed in nearby Strachur St but fortunately it didn't explode. Our building gave a frightening shudder when a German plane crashed on the Campsie hills on a cold winter's night. It was clearly visible the next day. Lambhill Ironworks, with a large workforce engaged in munitions work, was probably a prime target for air attack, as was the army camp at Blackhill, both in close proximity to the canal.

Baffie Walls

My earliest memories of World War Two were the baffle walls which were erected about three feet from the close mouth to prevent bomb blast. They were built 12 feet high and a foot thick and completed within a day. A local man worked long hours in the building trade and visited Mallon's to 'top-up' before closing time. When he emerged from the pub with his vision impaired, but in a jovial mood, he couldn't find his way into the close. He was grateful after being negotiated into the close. A sobering experience.

Some local men visited the Kenmure Arms or Mallon's for their weekend sustenance and social exchange, which on some occasions would have disastrous results come 9pm closing, but was often very entertaining for the local community.

On one particular summer evening, big Alec McDonald, all 6ft 4in of miner's bulk, and his wee brother, 6ft 2ins of miner's bulk, were having a fierce argument at closing time and decided to settle the argument in the traditional manner.

Followed by numerous locals they made their way to the grass verge beside the red stone house opposite the pub. The bare-knuckle battle commenced with both parties stripped down to their John L. Sullivan underwear. Miners worked hard and fought hard. Although both contestants were anaesthetised, it continued for over an hour before the contest was eventually declared a draw, with the contestants shaking hands. Both walked down Lambhill towards the terminus, arms wrapped around each other's shoulders, the reason for the bloodied exchange completely forgotten. Everyone parted amicably.

The highlight of the week was Saturday night at Wee Aggie's dancing. Girls were seated at one side of the hall and boys on the other. Dessy Struthers, the cheery MC, would scatter slippereen over the floor before the mad rush to grab a partner, especially if it was a Marina quick step. The music stopped and you had to kiss your partner. A Ladies Choice could be a bit risky until one of my sisters came to the rescue.

Dessy would lead off the eagerly-awaited Empress Tango and instruct the punters. *Two forward, two back.* We all became experts for life. Happy days at the local Lambhill dancing!

Football was dominant in Lambhill life which was played morning, noon and night, either at the red blaes park and the big lawn, or St Agnes's black ash park, and the wee lawn.

When important games were in progress, spectators had a wonderful view of the proceedings from high ground which dominated both football fields. The Boys' Guild football team was a big influence in athletic youth development, especially for ambitious individuals to attain a professional football career.

Barney Dunn was a well-known Lambhill worthy who had a small holding on the canal bank which included a nanny goat on a long rope as a deterrent to local weans. He raised his big, strapping family on the gantry behind Baird's cafe which had a cold water trough outside the window. His eldest son, Willie Dunn, had a successful spell with Celtic. Joe, Sam and Peter Dunn played

Springburn United football team

St Agnes' Boys Guild football team

for the famous Springburn United which also included Tommy Ring and Danny and John McGeachy from Lambhill. Almost all of them progressed to professional football.

Joe Wilkinson was a tall, impressive goalkeeper and the first priest to be born and raised in Lambhill, followed by George

Crawley whose family were originally from Springburn. His twin brother, Harry, was a stocky, tough defender who became a professional referee.

Harry Brannigan, a prolific centre-forward, and the ever-smiling, red-haired Tancy Lee, who would fly down the right wing, were memorable Boys Guild players. Some are still with us, such as John Gallagher the goalie and the ebullient Frank 'Thou Shall Not Pass' McCarron. He certainly took no prisoners! John and Billy McPhail, Tommy and Robert Bogan all nurtured their skills at Boys Guild level and were reared in Lambhill.

Veterans of the Guild continued to play the game with the same competitive spirit and were known as the 'Young Men'.

One particular game took place between the Young Men and Indian seamen from a ship berthed at King George V dock. Nine of these poor seamen played the whole game in their bare feet. One wore only socks and the eleventh man had borrowed baseball boots. The match was an ordeal for them, on a playing surface of nails, pieces of glass and wee stones.

What they lacked in footwear and footwork didn't take away from their commitment. The final result was of no consequence but a day of goodwill and fun was had by all.

Many an epic battle was fought on St Agnes's park between teams from all over the city, watched by hundreds of spectators. Some of the battles continued after the game had finished, between rival supporters. On the odd occasion some hotheads, incensed with the refereeing decisions, would surround the terrified official, bodily carry him shoulder-high over the stepping stones at the wide part of the burn and dump the poor soul in the canal. They would then help him out and up the bank to safety. Exciting days in peaceful, quiet Lambhill!

Men from Garscube Rd and Possil had the odd fisticuffs sessions after the pubs closed on Saturday night but when they played football in Lambhill on Sundays, with their big, heavy working boots, quite often for five shillings a man, they did so with great skill and good humour. These games were always trouble free. Lambhill United achieved great success under the management of Willie Denholm and Mr. Ferguson. Their home games were played at the red blaes park at the canal. Many of these fine footballers practised their skills at Possil High School. Jack Steedman from Haywood St was a silky passer in the big lawn and went on to play for Ashfield and Partick Thistle but reverted back to Junior football.

In the early fifties, Lambhill Amateurs were founded and included many good players; Danny Haggerty, Tom Loudon, Alec Brash and Hugh Brownlee the goalie, who had a wee puff at his fag in-between saves, and the three bustling Thorn brothers. Alec Thorn played centre-forward like a man possessed in his thirst for goals. Sometimes the ball and the opposing defender landed in the back of the net in no uncertain fashion. Probably working with horses made them strong and fearless. The Evening News sports section published the following article in 1954

THOM HITS 100 GOALS

Juniors Want Wee Alec. And His Mates

SAYS MALCOLM MUNRO

A FIRST-SEASON team, Lambhill Amateurs, members of the Glasgow Amateur League, have lost only one game. They're so good that every lad on the club's books is a potential Senior or Junior.

Ashfield are interested in centre-half Bobby Finlay. So is a Senior club. Right-half Tom Loudon has been out with Ashfield and the chances are the Saracen folks may do some business.

Wee Alec Thorn, sturdy, hard-hitting centre-forward, has banged home more than 100 goals this season.

He is one of five footballing Thorn brothers. Twins Sam and George made the Senior grade. Sam Joined Huddersfield and George, St Mirren.

Joe is still in the forces but will probably sign for Lambhill when he gets demobbed. Baby Colin at 16 is reckoned the brightest star of the lot. He is with the Hugh McGowan under-agers as an outside-left. The Lambhill Amateurs are in the semi-finals of the Glasgow Cup and the Glasgow Challenge Cup and top the league. A case of local boys and local team making good.

Sunday football was a regular event with lads from Milton and continued for years at the black ash park. These games were always good-natured fun with many outstanding players. In particular, from Milton, Archie Grant, Brian Callan, the Findley brothers, Robert, Jimmy and Willie Ross, Billy Lewis and big Tommy McKinnell, James McDermott, Olly Phinn, big John Fitzpatrick, Donnie McDowall, Billy Brash and Willie Yuill. I also recall many boyhood friends from Lambhill: Jack Gray, Billy Bain, Tommy Ross and Billy McConnechy, James and George Carlin, Jim Simpson, the red-headed twins James and John Collins and their young brother Frank. When drilling took place in the summer of 1961 for the construction of Balmore Industrial Estate, a way of life had come to an end.

The Flitting

After endless pleading with our local councillor, my mother secured a new house in Milton. We were leaving the Black Building in Lambhill full of happy memories for a new life in a new house. Without a backward glance we flitted in our uncle's horse and cart with all our goods and chattels the short distance to our new address along the unfinished street. This form of transportation was not uncommon in 1948.

In the fifties, a family was flitting from Possil to Cadder and by that time transportation had progressed from the horse and cart to the more modern open-back long lorry. When the contents were placed on the lorry, the wife supervised the operation with great pride by positioning each item as it would be in her new house. A kind of dress rehearsal. The settee at one side, two armchairs opposite with the standard lamp in between and, of course, the fire surround as the focal point with the husband comfortably ensconced on the settee reading the evening paper!

Possil Loch and Marsh

Its approximately 70-acre site is a barrier to any future building development, and at present is under the management of the Scottish Wildlife Trust. Opposite the preserved Lambhill Cemetery archway entrance is the beginning of a pleasant walk around the Marsh. In later years it was realised how important this forbidden area is to bird watchers and wildlife enthusiasts. Possil Loch and Marsh is an area three miles north from Glasgow city centre and a short distance from the Lambhill canal bridge.

Lambhill Community Council

The Marsh upgrading began when Lambhill Community Council provided help and premises to the Scottish Wildlife Trust in preparing and carrying out the new management plan and restoring the site to its present status. In response to the Job Creation Programme of June 1976, Lambhill Community Council prepared a programme of canal upgrading from Stockingfield to Bishopbriggs which was submitted by Jim Craigen MP to the job creation committee in Manpower Services. Lambhill CC was unable to carry out the programme but the concept was eventually incorporated into the reclamation proposals of the area. This organisation was created in 1977 and was successful in saving the former St Agnes's Primary in Balmore Rd from closure by a combined usage programme with Lambhill Nursery which was renamed Lambhill Village Hall. The premises were officially opened by Lord Provost David Hodge, a local man, in October 1979.

Throughout their 21 years as a community council, the long list of initiatives makes very impressive reading. Provision was made for local youth involvement in a wide range of activities. There has been Saracen Crime Prevention, Northern Alcoholics Anonymous and clubs for disabled. There have been health and educational opportunities, local interest for environmental improvement and awareness and a club for older residents in the district.

Lambhill Village Hall was a facility for many happy social gatherings, particularly those associated with the gala and school art programmes, which enjoyed great success over the years. All the local schools contributed to the development of the countless activities, with many dedicated individuals giving their time and talent. The list is endless of what took place and it is thanks to all the hard work done by the dedicated founding members such as Harry Dempsey, J.P. (Justice of the Peace), Gerald Byrne, Bill Taylor, Celia Irvine, Mary Harvey, Lily Telfer, Joe Barrie and his wife Helen. Not forgetting the many council members, including, sad to say, quite a number now deceased, who, over the years, gave of their time willingly for the people of Lambhill.

After the break-up of Strathclyde Region, Glasgow City Council became responsible for the school and halls building. In October 1998, the Lambhill and District Community Council's lease of the premises was terminated.

The Forth and Clyde Canal

In years gone by the canal area was used much more as an industrial waterway. In the thirties and early war period it remained an important waterway link. Materials were transported in long horse-drawn barges which passed through Lambhill to the Firhill

Basin and Speirs Wharf with tar, timber and coal. The barge usually had two of a crew, one man operating the tiller and his mate leading the trace-horse, preventing the animal making frequent stops to munch the grass.

Over many years the canal has been a neglected amenity abandoned to vandals and an area of discarded waste. Many volunteer groups have given their time to remedy the situation.

Although the canal was closed to boating in 1961, the Forth and Clyde Canal Society was formed in 1980. Its specific aim was to develop and restore the canal as a recreational feature of community life in all areas. Funding was granted by the European Commission as a Millennium Project. The Forth and Clyde Canal was re-opened on a memorable sunny Saturday June 24, 2001.

Church and School

St Agnes's

Generations of families from Lambhill and Possil have their own memories of St Agnes's school which was both 'primary' and 'advanced division'. Some with happy, others not so happy memories. Looking back, most people would agree that all the teachers taught with great diligence, influenced many of their charges and deserve to be remembered. Johnny O'Conner, Mrs. Wilkinson, Misses Rogers, Barrett and O'Neill, and Miss Heron, the Art teacher. Mr. Burns was the headmaster.

In the advanced division, I can only recall the inseparable Mr. Riddell, Mr. McMann and Mr. McNab. As written earlier in the narrative, the Black Building gable end was part of the school and the residents had a clear view of activity within and outwith school hours. When the janitor was absent, the playground was used by the locals for doublers, football, hide and-seek, or walking on the slippery peripheral wall. When Mrs. Wilkinson, from two up in the Red

Building, spotted me shimmying up the rone pipe to retrieve the ball on the school roof, I would be summoned to her house for a severe ticking off. Plans for the building and ground area by developers never came to fruition. The once-fine building lay derelict for many years due to age and dilapidation until vandals set fire to it and, sadly, St Agnes's old school was demolished at the beginning of June 2002.

History

The original school and school house were built in 1880 and the parish was opened in 1883 by Fr Houlihan from the Maryhill Mission. He rented a room at Cambus Villa in Crawford St (Knapdale St).

St Agnes's parish was created in 1884. Local miners cleared the site for the new church which was opened in 1893. The school became a combined school and chapel. In order to accommodate more children, the school chapel was enlarged and included a belfry in 1886. The centenary celebrations were memorable with many old parishioners coming back to Lambhill for the great event and reuniting with many residents who have remained in the area.

Lambhill Evangelical Church

The Lambhill Mission, as it was known locally, was originally held in the old Lambhill canal building by the canal bridge and was associated from about 1870 with the Maryhill V.F. Church. In 1906, Robert McLean, William Millar, James and John Ferguson, Alex and Colin Gibb, William Middleton, Alex McGhee, Matthew Brash, Sam Wilson, James and John Alexander met to inaugurate the New Mission leading to the new Mission Hall built by local effort in 1907 at Knapdale St.

The Mission was renamed 'The Lambhill Evangelical Church' in 1975 and is still going strong and well attended in all its activities.

St Agnes' church

Lambhill Gospel Band

The band of the Lambhill Mission made its first appearance in 1895. Although celebrating its centenary in 1995, the band was actually started in 1873 when William Middleton joined with Thomas McFarlane, William Crawford and William Millar to start the Lambhill Gospel Band. Other members at different times in-

Mission Hall, Knapdale St

cluded Jack and Jock Alexander, Harry and Colin Anderson, Dan Craig, Willie Gillies, George Hogg, Henry and Ronnie Paul, Jack Armstrong, John and Robert Glen, Dan Muir, James Middleton, Colin Gibb, Norman White and many others who gave their time and skill in the service of the band. As well as providing church music, innumerable open-air performances have been given over the years, often on Saturdays at the foot of Knapdale St and in Cadder; also at the popular Sunday School trips at which they often marched to Possilpark station to catch the excursion train. All in all, a most dedicated and exhilarating piece of local life.

There is a unique bond which exists with folk from Lambhill which is both sentimental and nostalgic and not just a yearning for the past but of many fond memories forged when life in the district had a number of communities under the umbrella of Lambhill.

POSSIL

Introduction

When Terry Welsh told me he was preparing a book on Old Possil I was delighted and curious. Delighted because it is past time for such a book and because it may be the last chance to tap the memories of Old Possilites. Curious, because I couldn't wait to see what would be forthcoming.

Well, here it is, and it is well worth the wait. I guess the folk in Possil will queue up to grab this little volume, not just for themselves but for all the ex-Possilites now far off in America, Canada ... and East Kilbride. Terry kindly asked me for a contribution which I was happy to give. Well done Terry, you have opened a treasure house of memories.

Bill Taylor

Present-day Possilpark, geographically, has seen very little change since the pre-war period. The main artery is Saracen St which is the heart of Possil with its busy shopping centre.

Although Possil now has a tarnished reputation and has been described as a socially deprived and drug-related area resulting in the tragic loss of many young lives, older residents and people from the surrounding districts have fond memories of the Possil of old. Before World War Two and on into the early post-war period, there was plenty of work for everyone. On reflection, this densely populated community was hard-working and respectable. There was a wide variety of light and heavy industry in the Possil area and its periphery.

Saracen Foundry

The world-renowned MacFarlane's Saracen Foundry employed a large workforce where men would emerge after a hard day's graft as black as the ace of spades. There were no facilities for washing or changing for the workers. If they had to go home by public transport, other passengers would give them a wide berth. MacFarlane made a gift to the local community of a bandstand, a water trough for horses (situated outside Smart's pub at the Cross) and the street-drinking fountain with the chained iron cup outside the Balmore pub in Balmore Rd. They also donated

Saracen Foundry

the site for Possilpark Library which was built on a Carnegie grant. They manufactured a variety of products for worldwide distribution including ornamental ironwork, rainwater pipes and guttering, balustrades and many types of architectural ironwork. Many of their designs can still be seen in different districts of Glasgow.

A.J. Mains, the steelworks situated in Hawthorn St at Ashfield St, was the usual noisy steelworks with the very distinctive red-leaded smell. At the end of the shift, some workers removed their dungarees stiff with paint and stood them in a corner. You could say they were freestanding!

Bells' Pottery

The Glasgow Pottery factory in Denmark St was founded by two brothers, John and Matthew Perston Bell. They employed a good number of female workers and produced an assortment of items in porcelain and earthenware throughout their manufacturing history. Locally, it was always referred to as Bells' Pottery. Before its demise, hot-water bottles known as piggies were made in the Denmark St premises. Unlike the steelworks on the opposite side of the road, which had its huge doors always wide open, the Pottery had its doors closed to the prying eyes of the locals. The carters quite often loaded their wagons from a hole in the wall. This particular factory started trading around the 1875 period and was known originally as the Saracen Pottery. At a later date it was renamed the Possil Pottery and finally closed its doors in 1948 as Bells' Pottery.

At the foundry end of Hawthorn and Denmark St was the fibreglass works, a subsidiary of Pilkington Glass, which opened its doors in 1948. Unfortunately, the operation was closed down in 1970 with the loss of 500 jobs. Yet another blow to the people of Possilpark.

Mosshouse

The other end of Denmark St was Brownlee and Murray's steel-works and the dreaded School Dental Clinic. The free dinner school was at the corner of Bardowie and Denmark St. During World War Two, under certain requirements breakfast, dinner and tea were free. Behind the Mosshouse – a solitary building situat-ed at the junction of Possil Rd and Saracen St – was Brownlee's Sawmill, a site later occupied by the Alliance Box Company (now closed).

White Horse Whisky Bond

At the Mosshouse, a large number of girls dressed in their tur-bans and overalls cheerfully made their way home from the White Horse Whisky Bond to different parts of Possil. There was more than met the eye with regard to dress and behaviour for the girls employed there. The turban played a major role in the pecking order of the shop-floor culture.

Lone worker at the whisky bond

Whisky bond production line

Although there was no monetary gain or advantage inherent to the dress, certain codes of practice had to be diligently adhered to. In the bottling hall, all the women had to wear white overalls and a white turban which was a triangular piece of cloth. The part you fulfilled in these operations determined how you wore your turban. The bottling hall was a large spacious area consisting of numerous conveyor-belt systems. At the top end of the line was the bottling machine in which the whisky was decanted into bottles which emerged from an adjoining hall.

The next stage in the operation was the important task of scrutinising for any possible impurities. After this rigorous inspection by two girls, the bottles were conveyed to the labelling machines, dusted and sent further down the line to be wrapped in white tissue paper and eventually packed in cardboard boxes each containing 12 bottles of 'the water of life'.

Boxes were then sealed and stacked ready for dispatching. Some of the hard stuff was given special treatment and added protection. A consignment was placed in wooden cases and wire wrapped by teams of two girls. They enjoyed a privileged position in the pecking order. Packers and wirers also wore leather protective aprons over their white overalls with great pride as this was the ultimate status symbol. Girls performing some of the more mundane tasks wore their turbans in such a particular fashion that it resembled a cap as all of the ends of the triangular headpiece were neatly tucked in. Those with some status – packers and wirers – displayed their turbans in such a way that they were easily recognised by the entire workforce as having the most difficult and strenuous jobs in the factory. In retrospect, it seems strange that a large number of workers aspired to these lofty positions as only pride in achievement was involved.

The Askit Factory

In Saracen St at Killearn St, the Askit pharmaceutical works was a familiar landmark in Possil. The staff were mostly female and instantly recognisable, dressed in their clinically white overalls. At the rear of the Askit building was Harper's sweetie works.

Smith's Engineering

The top end of Killearn St was always referred to as the Red Building end. Beyond these wally closes was the world famous Smith's Engineering. When the low-loader vehicle arrived, their massive doors would reveal a huge turbine ready for transportation to the docks. On the opposite side was a small cluster of prefabs constructed during the war as temporary housing. Schweppes soft drinks factory was also in Killearn St for many years.

Blind Asylum

John Leitch, a Glasgow man, donated the sum of £5,000 to found a charitable institution for the blind in 1804. He himself suffered partial blindness in later life. The original BA workshop was opened at Castle St in 1828 and moved to Saracen St before the beginning of World War Two when the building became an extension of the Royal Infirmary.

The Blind Asylum building, which was previously Greenlees shoe factory, dominated that part of Saracen between Killearn St and Stonyhurst St. The BA consisted of six floors and was a hive of productivity. Bedding, leather work, brushes, floor mats and baskets were produced here and basket weaving was considered a most specialised skill. All the products were displayed at the ground-floor office complex.

James Cowan, the author of 'From Glasgow's Treasure Chest', visited the Blind Asylum in Saracen St in 1939 and stated: "It is the largest industrial workshop for the blind in the world. When I left this wonderful place, it was not with a feeling of depression as I feared I might. Instead, I realised that, apart from my own feeling of sadness at seeing so many sightless faces, I had neither seen or heard any sign of gloom among these hundreds of workers. In every department where the work admitted of it, there was always a cheerful buzz of conversation, and often quite a lot of singing, and good singing, too; and in every case the work was obviously being done with a zest that carried its own enjoyment."

Many talented, skilful men and women worked in the BA. In some departments a number of workers had a 'blink' (people with partial sight) and they performed work compatible with their limited sight. Female workers considered these descriptions derogatory and would have preferred to be referred to as having limited vision or partially sighted. The men didn't seem to mind. When in full production, the boot and shoe repair flat mended over 500 pairs on a weekly basis. Conditions in the BA left a lot to be desired.

It was common knowledge amongst the workforce that they had the lowest grade of wages of all council employees. A police constable was always present at the front door at lunchtime and finishing time at 5pm. When the finishing whistle sounded, the whole of Saracen came to a standstill to enable the workers to be transported to various parts of the city. During the fifties and sixties, the BA employed over 500 workers.

In days gone by the binmen emptied the middens at night. The long, silent motor had flaps and a running board on either side of the vehicle. Midden men would emerge from the rear, miners' lamps on their caps, and carrying huge, strong wicker baskets on their backs to empty the bins. These baskets were manufactured in the Blind Asylum.

Tram at the Blind Asylum

Beyond Saracen Cross on Balmore Rd at Sunnylaw St was a small building which was called the Nougat Work. Only a small workforce was employed and comprised of seven or eight girls and one man who operated the machinery to produce wafers, snowballs, sponges and, of course, nougats.

Woodside Engineering

Known locally as the 'nut and bolt factory', this plant occupied a large site between Stronend St and Mireton St on the busy Balmore Rd. The factory had a large, mixed personnel but was predominately staffed by female workers. They wore dark dungarees similar to the men.

Tramcars

Possilpark tram depot provided employment for a large number of people. In addition to the all-important green staff, there

Greenlees factory

were maintenance personnel and the cleaners known as the black squad.

There was a nucleus of tram drivers who proudly wore 30 and 40-year service badges with the cherished hope of the ultimate promotion to the rank of inspector and obtaining the wee hat. Many will recall those kindly drivers – wearing wooden clogs, big gloves and stamping their feet on winter days – who would agree to take linoleum and drum kits on board and chat to you in the family department upstairs where the conductors leaned out of the window to reset the 'bow collector'. If someone was caught between tram stops and thought it was possible to jump on, it became a challenge that had to be executed with expert timing. When the driver spotted anyone running alongside his tram, nine times out of ten he would slow down to let him board. Occasionally some younger drivers would go faster at the precise moment you launched yourself aiming for the centre pole on the platform. You grabbed it tightly with both hands and usually did a birlie three times round the pole, regained your dignity and took a seat with smug satisfaction.

The conductors took the job very seriously. All of the buttons were polished and the uniform was pressed to army standards. The women conductors could address any situation with authority and never missed a fare. She was the boss and knew all the dodges. "Plenty seats upstairs." One man once protested angrily, "Ave goat a widden leg!" "Them wi' widden legs doon stairs, able-bodies upstairs," came the reply. There was also: "Rheumatics inside, romantics upstairs," and "Git Aff! before a throw ye aff. Ah've goat ten stannin', that's ma limit".

It was a wonderful spectacle when the Coronation tram travelled through Possil, new and shiny, with the driver seated in his private cabin proud as punch. The majestic vehicle was introduced for George VI's coronation in 1937 and also transported passengers to the Empire Exhibition at Bellahouston Park in 1938.

Lambhill-bound tram at Paisley Road Toll

Two trams in Strachur St

Cafes

Joe's

Possil always had a selection of Italian cafes, Joe' s cafe in Saracen St being the most popular and usually busy most days. Joe was always immaculately dressed. He was a smiling, pleasant man but very strict regarding the customers. On Tuesdays he would proudly have his big American car parked at the cafe ready for the family outing. It was a great spectacle. Joe was a well-known figure in Possil over many years. Many people will be surprised to read that he lived to the age of 96. Many a romance started and blossomed over a Macallum in his cafe.

The Lido

On the opposite side of Saracen St, the Lido was always busy. The proprietors were very quiet people who worked hard to compete for business. There was a healthy rivalry between the Lido and

Joe's, which dissolved when George di Julius married Joe's eldest daughter Adeline. Both shops always maintained a high standard of cleanliness and quality. The glass gantry always had a nice display and the shop had highly polished mirrors. When Joe eventually retired, Violet, his middle daughter, would lend a hand in the Lido cafe. She had crossed the great divide.

Linardi's

Also in Saracen St was the spacious Copacabana which could cater for a large number of customers, especially after the services in St Teresa's or the Church of Scotland at Stonyhurst St.

Cafe Modern

Further along Saracen St at the tram points terminal, just beyond Bardowie St, was the Cafe Modern which was owned by two sisters. Everyone had their own preference, with plenty of choice as far as cafes were concerned.

Chippies

What about the chippies? People had their own particular favourite. May's at Mansion St was one of the best and was always very busy. It was common practice to bring along a large plate if you had a substantial order. The Balmore chip shop served lovely fish and chips and also the tasty, spicy VC (Vincent Coia) pies. This establishment always provided good, quick service and was owned by a nice, quiet Italian man. His four handsome assistants served at breakneck speed and were always very pleasant.

Saracen St with foundry in background

Pierotti

Children were attracted by the wee aquarium in the front window. The Churchillian figure of Mr. Pierotti was the boss of the only sit-in chippy in Possil, a great favourite with teenagers on a cold night. It was also popular with men emerging from the pub with a dose of central heating and in need of sustenance. Mrs. Pierotti was a popular figure in Possil. She had a charming way with young people and served the customers at those iron and marble-topped tables with great patience. Her shiny, wavy black hair, good looks and those long, dangling gold earrings have earned her a place in Possil folklore.

Night Star

The Night Star at Allander St and Barloch St was something else. This busy chip shop always seemed to be full of weans and dogs, all running about mad. It was the last outpost when you were hungry, as they didn't close till midnight.

Pompy's

Opposite the Pottery in Denmark St was Pompy's who specialised in delicious fritters. If you didn't have thruppence for chips, Pompy would make a wee funnel-type poke and give you three ha'pence worth of 'scrapins'. It was a great treat in those days. Life was simple then.

Barbers

Mignano's

The Mignano family arrived in Possilpark in 1937. Mr. Mignano and his brother Rico set up business at the Hawthorn St end of Saracen St opposite Waddell's cycle shop. A couple of years later, they moved along near to the tram-points terminal, close to Saracen Cross and opened a ladies and gents' hairdressers. Mr. Mignano was a wee dapper Italian barber, always well dressed and wearing rimless glasses. The ladies' section was situated at the front of the shop. As the gents' section was in the rear, men and boys in for the usual short-back-and-sides had to negotiate their way through the ladies' section in dignified silence.

Remember those hair clippers? If that machine contacted a spot in the back of your neck en route to the top of your head, it was murder. There were dozens of wee boys walking about Possil with a can-can fringe at the front and the rest of the head shaved into the wood. That was the style preferred because you then wouldn't need a haircut for a long time. All the men had their heads shaved at the back, just like Peter 'Ma Baw' McKennan.

He was over 6ft and a personality player with Partick Thistle for many years.

All the Mignano family were employed in the business at one time or another and also Mr. Mignano's brother Rico, who was a popular figure in Possil over many years. Rico never quite captured the Glasgow accent. He was a lovely, friendly man and had survived four years of internment during the World War Two. He would say, "How-a-much-you-a-want-a-off?" and would then proceed to give his philosophy lesson. With his gentle application of the scissors, it was difficult to stay awake. Rico could cut hair in jig-time and then he would say, "Who-sa-next-please?" He was known to partake of one or two wee 'goldies' (half of whisky) on the odd occasion and would then become vociferous. He became more Italian than Pavarotti but never attained Pavarottian proportions. He still looked dapper in his final years and is the only man known to keep his tobacco roll-ups in a silver cigarette case. Rico always had style. He died aged 92. Eddie Mignano is the only member of his family at present involved in the family business where he had started as a 14-year-old boy.

The business is still operating in the same premises, uninterrupted since the late thirties. Recently Eddie was recalling how as a young boy, he was sent to Renucci's Italian bakery in Bardowie St to collect pizza, which of, course was only known to the Italian community at that time. The Rainbow's End (Cossar's) cafe in Balmore Rd on the opposite side of the one-time Possil Secondary School was a popular haunt for teenagers. The owners installed a jukebox, which was the latest rage from America. It was a big, yellow machine, all glass and shiny. If you fed the thing a sixpence it would play your favourite tune. Eventually the thing broke down. Pete Murray, from Possil, a dab hand at the guitar, suggested to Eddie Mignano who was proficient on the clarinet, that they perform in Cossar's cafe on Sundays. They went down a treat. Eddie was dressed in the 'full drape', wearing crepe sole shoes and Glenn Miller specs. Everyone consumed gallons of orange juice and danced to live music.

Grant's

This barbers in Saracen St had its own routine and was very busy. The customers were squeezed in like sardines. Folk were shunted from the door in assembly-line fashion and thrust out into Saracen St still smarting from those deadly hair clippers. It was worse than the Denmark St dentist!

Sporting Life

Glasgow Perthshire Football Club was formed by a small group of business men from Perth who had settled in Glasgow in the 1880s.

Their intention was to form a cricket club. In 1890, they chose to establish a football club. The first ground was in Maryhill at Oran St and at a later date moved to Balmore Park opposite Balmore Square at Balmore Rd, close to the junction at Hawthorn St. They settled in Keppoch Park at Ashfield St in 1932 and, like their close neighbours Ashfield, won many trophies with great personalities from football legend. Both clubs always had a number of local lads on the books such as Dick and John Flood, two red-headed brothers. There was also Alec Murphy, who was an efficient, skilful centre-half, and Davy Clements, an aggressive left-back. Gus McAlpine and Willie Findley were also prominent players as were many others too numerous to mention who wore the Perthshire colours with distinction.

Ashfield Juniors were founded in 1886 and have produced many fine players throughout their illustrious history. This would not have been possible without the calibre of dedicated and

Ashfield Juniors football team

far-sighted individuals who have been associated with this club all their lives. One individual who deserves a special mention was the legendary Davy Collins – 'Mr. Ashfield' – who had a lifelong connection with the club. There are endless stories about Davy and his commitment to football. He was on gate duty in 1921 when he confronted the great Alec James and told him: "This is the players' entrance. The boys' gate is next door." In the 1952-3 season, Ashfield were having a successful run in the Junior Cup and playing in front of six and seven thousand spectators. A home game against Clydebank Juniors, with Joe Roy their baldy, classy inside-forward dominating play, produced a classic. Wee McCarthy at inside left for Ashfield was playing a stoatir. He had an educated left foot and wasn't the size of tuppence. John Divers, another small player with silky skills, was at inside right. Jimmy Robb was an athletic keeper, only 5ft 8ins, small for a goalie. The key player, Rankin Black, was a prolific centre-forward. In the second half, Rankin received a bad injury to his left leg and left the field for treatment. On his return, to everyone's surprise, his right leg was bandaged and he played the remainder of the game on the left wing. Ashfield won that day and everything else that season.

They were a wily and crafty bunch. Possilpark and district produced a wealth of football talent due to the dedication of the remarkable Bobbie Dinnie.

He discovered Kenny Dalglish and Jim Watt who were members of Possil YMCA Although Watt became famous in boxing, he showed early promise as a footballer. Charlie McKenna, a well-known figure in football circles, was a strong left-half with Hamilton Accies; he has total recall and can name so many famous footballers from the Possilpark area.

Joe Jackson played for Bolton. George Brown played for Rangers and was also capped for Scotland. There was Joe Feeney, Jim Shields, Eddie Kelly, Alec Massey, and Joe McColgan. Alec Rollo was a powerful full-back with Celtic and, of course, Bertie Auld played for Panmure Thistle. Wee John Divers played for Clyde when they lifted the Scottish Cup after beating Celtic in a replay. Tommy Ring was another outstanding footballer. His unique skills on the left wing with Clyde earned him many caps for his country.

It was amazing that football players in times gone by showed such dexterity and skill when you consider the 'bladder' was made of leather panels with an inner tube tucked inside. After the inner tube was inflated, the neck was carefully folded under the opening and tightly laced. The ball was a ton weight when the weather was wet and the ground heavy. Some wag would shout, "Cross the ba' wi' the lace oan the ootside". There were always fierce football games at Cowlairs. If a tense match was being played at one of the pitches at the clinic end, you could put the pot on for one of the players to blooter the ball out the park as far as Carlyle St, which took about 10 minutes to retrieve. On a summer's evening, hundreds watched football at the sloping park in Saracen St which was the site for the Barrage Balloon at the start of World War Two. Massive searchlights were positioned at the highest point in Cowlairs Park. It was an exciting spectacle.

Speedway

This new sport, introduced and organised by Johnny Hoskins, was highly successful. Ashfield Giants were created in 1947 with such famous personalities as Ken Le Breton, who wore white leathers and was immediately christened 'The White Ghost'. He was the big favourite with the fans because of his courage and daring skills. Merv Harding also enjoyed a huge following of fans with his good looks and flamboyant style. Le Breton was killed while racing in Australia in 1950. Speedway lost its appeal in the early fifties but Possil people remember with great affection when it was great entertainment for many from all age groups. During its heyday, 'Cycle Speedway' became a popular sport with teenagers. Bicycles were stripped for lightness, speed and manoeuvrability. Teams from different areas of the city competed with courage and skill to emulate their Speedway favourites.

Continental Boules

Throughout the summer Sunday evenings, a popular pastime with the Italian community was the Boules. The venue for these gatherings was the spare ground at the dummy railway between Balmore Rd and Bilsland Dr Fierce arguments and much gesticulating took place with the usual Italian temperament, which was great fun for the spectators sitting on the embankment.

Ashfield Club

In the early sixties period, Jimmy Donald, a local bookmaker, opened the Ashfield Club. Glen Daly (Bartholomew Dick, often described as 'Mr Glasgow') became the resident showbusiness personality. Glen was a rabid Celtic supporter and worked for many years with Lex McLean in the Pavilion, who didn't conceal his Blue Nose affiliation. Glen's record, 'The Celtic Song', when first recorded in the 60s, sold over a million copies. Even today it is still being played in the new Celtic stadium. Hector Nicol was also a popular stand-up comic at the Ashfield Club. His brand of jokes and humour were a bit blue and near the bone. He was from the east coast and went down a treat with the ladies. Billy Connolly appeared at the beginning of his solo comedian career in the Ashfield Club perhaps with the help of Glen Daly. Both of them had been shipyard welders, benefiting from the characters and Glasgow humour which is renowned the world over.

Going to the Pictures

The 'Wee Possil' picture hall in Saracen St was magic. After presenting the 'jam jaur' or 'jeely jaur' (which had to be clean) at the door, you then entered the war zone. Hundreds of screaming weans having a great time at the matinee on a Saturday afternoon. After the frenzy on Saturdays, the usherettes must have swallowed a few Askit powders after their work.

The Mecca in Balmore Rd was upmarket and very plush. After a long wait in the pouring rain, the customers were ushered into the foyer – real fancy. Mrs. Staunton or Jeanie Ward would issue your ticket and you had to wait in another queue. The usher, in full uniform regalia, would shout, "Two singles and a double". If eligible for one of these vacancies, this meant that you were led to the wooden barrier, behind the "winchers" back stalls, just in time for the community singing. "You are my sunshine, my only sunshine, you make me happy, when skies are grey." Everybody singing like linties giving it big licks. We were easily pleased, or just plain daft.

Possil Life

Pawnshops

Quigley's Pawn in Bardowie St and McManus's Pawn in Balmore Rd were a necessary means of survival at the beginning of the week whenever people found themselves short of cash.

A large number of families depended on these establishments to provide money for the bare necessities of life until pay day. If the pawn was frequented, it was kept a secret. Approaching those hallowed premises, the routine was to pause for a few minutes, keek round the corner and make sure that no one in the vicinity recognised you, and when the coast was clear you could then make a beeline for the entrance. You then entered the dark interior hoping to find an empty cubicle as quickly as possible. The saloon-type door always had creaky hinges and made a loud bang. That was the signal for the pawnbroker to approach your cubicle and commence the duel regarding the price. He always won this psychological war. On pay day, or whenever it was possible to redeem these items, usually a suit or coat, the pawnbroker would carefully wrap them in a large sheet of brown paper. The game was a bogey. Everyone knew you had come from the pawn.

The Co-op

The Co-operative store in Saracen St was a way of life for countless families. When the Divy (Dividend) was due, it was an opportunity to clear some outstanding debt. People loved the atmosphere of the Co. It was a place to meet neighbours and friends. Some of the products were in canvas bags on the sawdust floor. Sugar was scooped into thick, brown bags and deftly folded and sealed. A big French loaf shaped like Gibraltar was a weekend treat. If it was cut thickly and spread with good butter or treacle it was described as a 'sore haun'. Bread was uncut and customers would bring a cloth or a pillow slip to wrap it in. Raisins, currants, nuts and peas were bagged with great speed and humour. Somebody would give you a poke in the ribs and shout, "That's your number being called". Everyone's 'Co' number was tattooed into their brain from an early age, never to be forgotten. In today's world, most adults over a certain age could recite their number without the slightest hesitation.

Sadly, all of the old shops have disappeared: Massey's, Curley's and Forrester's stores – which was also an advice centre – McFarlane's gents' drapers, Methven's sweetie shop. Smith's fruit shop remains at the same location, under different owners. The Co-operative is still trading in Possilpark, situated behind Saracen Cross in Bardowie St. Next to the 'Co' was Sammy Devine's fruit shop which did a roaring trade selling a whole range of goods and was open for business after all other shops had closed. On Christmas Eve he sold Christmas trees until midnight. Cossar's bakery and many others too numerous to mention, have gone. Many Possil people remember big Alec's wee shop at Barloch St and Stonyhurst St. Alec owned a piggery and encouraged local children to bring a bag of brock in exchange for sweeties. This practice went on for years.

War Years

At the beginning of World War Two, many families had to struggle to survive under extreme conditions, in many cases as a one-parent family. Rationing quickly became a way of life. The war created a whole new culture and language; leg tan and peroxide blondes. Some of the expressions weren't always complimentary such as "She's goat a face like a torn melodeon" or, for some poor soul with a squint, "He's goat wan eye in the pot an wan eye up the chimney". When a person sounded pretentious, or if vanity was observed, "She fancies her barra," was the refrain. People had to cope with a different environment - the blackout and the ARP, rationing and running helter skelter for the shelters.

Room with a View

Tenement life evokes affection and fond memories of life 'up our close'. People living in close proximity to each other created a unique atmosphere; Sharing a communal toilet, the obligatory turn at the stairs and beating the hell oot the one carpet over the clothes rope in the back court; Fragile gas mantles and, of course, the big range which had to be blackened, especially if visitors were expected. "Hingin' oot the windae" was a feature of tenement life for some who lived up a close. To have a 'hing' meant usually leaning on a pillow with arms folded, in a comfortable position, watching the world go by. Before telephones or television, this habit was a commercial break from the household chores. From the lofty perch, 'leaning out the windae' was an important means of communication. Children could be summoned immediately to go a wee message. Disputes could be settled or a neighbour would stop at the close for a chat. Some people in the close liked to 'keep to themselves'. If that was the case, the communication was very polite and formal. Another advantage of a 'hing' was that a local character called wee Harry could be spotted from a distance selling bunches of sticks. Everything about Harry was wee. He sold his firewood from a wee horse and cart. He sat on a wee box smoking his wee pipe and wore a wee bunnet and scarf. He had a wee place in Bardowie St. He was a wee, enterprising business man. Usually another horse and cart would appear after Harry, loaded with steaming coal briquettes, which sold like hotcakes.

Housing in Possil, in comparison with many densely populated areas of the city, was mixed. The slum clearances, a low-

Barloch St, Henry Drummond church

er grade of intermediate and other intermediate housing were luxury compared with tenements. The 'Arches' in East Keppoch has been renovated in recent times and the only major housing development in the post-war period was the creation of Wester Common. Hamiltonhill has also been updated to meet the high standards of modern demands and housing legislation. After the war the priority was to re-house people in a healthy environment and so the large new conurbations and new towns were created.

Churches in Possilpark were numerous. Possilpark Parish Church in Ardoch St with their big cheery minister, Jim Hutcheson, catered for the youth with great vigour. Henry Drummond in Allander St at Barloch St, had an active large congregation and had been established over a long period.

St Teresa's church, old and new

Before his retirement, Mr. Hutcheson built the busy modern Rockvilla church in Saracen St, which is the only remaining Church of Scotland in the district. Mr. Hutcheson gave sterling service to his congregation for a total of 36 years and had great insight into the whole environment of Possil and its needs. St Teresa's in Saracen St was always 'standing-room only' at all the services. The parish embraced the whole area from the south-west end of Hawthorn St to the Mosshouse. The church was opened in 1932. Older parishioners remember with great affection the ever-popular Fr McCrory. Also, Frs. McLeod and McFaul, not forgetting the gentle-giant figure of Fr McKinnon and, of course, Fr Broderick, now retired. In recent times, Fr Nugent devoted his energies towards the youth of the area. Youth involvement was an integral part of church life in St Teresa's from the beginning. Boys' Guild football was well organised and has flourished since the thirties.

The Rag Man

Boys would always be on the lookout for shiny sticks or two shiny bones from the butchers to make 'clappers'. They were a prized possession. "Here's the Rag Man cummin", was the excited cry from the weans scurrying home to pester their mother. The Rag Man could be heard in the back court rattling his porcelain clappers with great skill. After coaxing your poor mother to make the bundle of rags as big as possible, you then proceeded to bargain for the balloon on the stick. It was a serious business. Quite often you had to settle for the candy rock. The Rag Man eventually replaced the plates with the bugle. What a helluva noise that was. It was neither Reveille nor the Last Post, more like the sound of a tug coming up the Clyde blasting a distress signal. He must have been a bugler on his granny's side.

Saracen Cross

For years, it was common practice for young men to stand at each corner of Saracen Cross. Some of the corner boys spent hours in Possil library and could argue on every subject under the sun. The police would disperse them from time to time until they had to attend the warning light on the police box at the toilets in Bardowie St. The police presence wasn't always evident in the district. The 'Black Maria' was in the area the odd Friday or Saturday, usually when the pubs were closing.

The west side of Saracen St was policed from the Maryhill station and the east side was serviced by Maitland St. The police station in Barloch St was opened in 1974 and at present is staffed with more than 100 personnel.

Dr Montgomery

When the much revered, and sometimes intimidating, tall and handsome figure of Dr Montgomery came into the house there was a reverential silence. This striking figure from Lewis had arrived in Possil in 1924 accompanied by Dr Balloch, after a brief spell in Garscube Rd. If he was attending a confinement he didn't waste any time. "I will need a basin of hot water and two dry towels," he commanded. After his examination he would carefully wash his hands and then inspect the whole family. "That is a whitlow you have on your finger. Come down to the surgery and have it lanced. Put a poultice on that boil (sugar and soap)." Many families were the beneficiaries of this practical and compassionate man. Among many kind acts little known to the general public, he paid for many bags of coal for his patients. It was not common knowledge that Dr Montgomery and Dr Balloch distributed food parcels to needy families. His half-crown fee on the mantelpiece, in many instances, was not uplifted. Home confinements were often considered preferable by families. Dr Montgomery could make as many as 40 house calls on a Sunday. He died in 1959 at the age of 65 and to the present day is remembered with great affection. He was a legend in his lifetime.

Dr Balloch shared the same reputation as her husband for her dedication to her patients and contribution to the welfare of the people in Possilpark. In fact, Dr Balloch was still in practice at the ripe old age of 80. This exceptional woman lived to the grand age of 96.

Dr Fitzsimmons and Dr O'Hagan

Both started in Garscube Rd before moving up to Possilpark where they remained until the late eighties. John Fitzsimmons had played professional football with Clyde and Celtic. He even-

Dr Montgomery

Dr Balloch with grandchild

tually held the position of team doctor to both the Celtic and Scottish teams. He had a very direct manner and a good memory for patients' names. His wife recalls the time when a woman patient called to see him, and for once his memory deserted him. "I know you," he said before blurting out, "I stitched you in Oakbank when you were drunk and fell down the stairs."

When that terrible disaster happened at Ibrox Stadium on stairway No.13 on the January 2, 1971, with the tragic loss of 66 lives, Dr Fitzsimmons worked tirelessly for the victims.

Facenna Family

This family have been associated with Possilpark for well over a century. Germano Facenna, the eldest son of a working-class family, left his native Italy to try and make a better living for his family. The young Germano arrived in Gosport, England, and although he did not write or speak English very well, he was a gifted man with his hands and was able to make almost

Mosshouse Rest cafe, owner in doorway

anything from wood or metal. He found work initially with his great love of horses, and by sheer hard work soon established himself while making concentrated efforts to improve his English, saving regularly until he was able to bring his family to a new life in England in 1875. With the support of his family, he got involved in the ice-cream business and flourished. After a few successful years, the family finally arrived in the Possil

The horsedrawn Facenna ice-cream van

area of Glasgow. Germano opened his first shop in Keppochhill Rd, the Pinkston Cafe, and then established a second shop, the Mosshouse Rest.

In those early days the two brothers started their working day at 4.30am preparing the ice cream. Around this period, several horse-drawn ice-cream vans were appearing in Glasgow. He introduced the first four-wheel cart in Scotland, which he had brought from London.

As more motor vehicles came on the scene, Germano's brother, Michael Angelo, introduced a motorcycle and sidecar vehicle and served the Hamiltonhill area for many years. Unfortunately, when the Second World War broke out the sons were conscripted, Germano closed the shops and retired. However, soon after the war, Angelo's son opened a garage business in Bardowie St and once again the business prospered.

After the untimely death of Angelo's son, his other sons, Michael and Gerry, took over the business. Trading as Ashfield Motors, they moved the company to the Colston area of Bishopbriggs. At the Colston headquarters the company achieved a first in Scotland with the introduction of the new Metrocab

Taxi, which was an alternative to the London Hackney cab. This vehicle, with provision for the disabled, caused some consternation when it first appeared on the streets of Glasgow. Some people thought it was a hearse. The traditional family business is now known as Allied Vehicles and is located in Lomond St industrial estate just a stone's throw from its origins, therefore maintaining their long association with Possilpark.

Taylor Family

Another prominent family involved in the early development of Possilpark was the Taylor family. Bill Taylor is its last local remaining member and has made the following contribution in his own words.

"My father, David Taylor, whose stories of the old days enthralled me as a boy, was born in Possilpark in 1887. Alec, my grandfather, and his brother Wull, were builders and moved their firm to Possil in 1883 when the building of the little town of Possilpark was underway. In 1868, John Campbell, of Possil, who owned Possil House and the estate, sold four plots and part of Keppoch farm to Walter McFarlane and his partners, engineers and ironfounders. During the next 10 years or so, the firm was engaged in setting out the ground for housing and commercial usages and for moving its factory from near the Saracen Head Inn to the new premises taking up the main area of old Possil House and grounds.

"The direct approach from the Mosshouse to the front gate was then named Saracen St. Sheriff Alison of Lanarkshire, a noted celebrity, was the last occupant of Possil House. Charles Dickens, who stayed with him on a visit, wrote to his friend Forster: 'Alison lives in style in a handsome country house out of Glasgow and is a capital fellow, with agreeable wife, nice little daughter, cheerful niece. All things pleasant in his household. Unbounded hospitality and 'enthoosywoozy' the order of the day and I have never been more heartily received anywhere or enjoyed myself more completely.' Not bad for Possil!

"The building programme in the close proximity to the foundry progressed at a steady rate. By the 1890s the population had risen to around 10,000. At this period, 1200 were employed in Saracen foundry. At this particular time, the Taylor business was fully occupied in various building contracts which included the doctor's house and surgery at Allander St and Saracen St. The first occupants were Dr Ross Muir and Dr Jope.

"The first phase of Old Possil school was started along with the Co-operative building and the three adjoining red sandstone tenements. Four tenements in Ardoch St stood opposite the school. Two tenements close to Possilpark Parish Church and Possil Library were also built by the family firm around this period. All this building activity took place before the First World War. In 1896 my grandfather fell from scaffolding at the building of Sommerville Church in Keppochill Rd. He was badly injured and was crippled for the remainder of his life. Dr Muir attended him at home. One day he said to him: 'Muir, when I finish my work it stands up for folk to see. When you're finished with yours it's clappit ower with a spade.'

"He died in 1903 at the early age of 56. We have a skiagraph, dated December 1896, taken of the injury to his leg. This is quite interesting in that it was taken by the first skiagraph or X-ray apparatus to be operated in the world which had just been introduced at the Glasgow Royal Infirmary in March of that year by Dr John Macintyre. Alex's great grandson, David, was one of the Diasonograph design team working with Professor Donald of the Queen Mother's, who were instrumental in producing the first practical electronic scanning machine for medical purposes. David's daughter was the first unborn child to appear on a prenatal scan on this machine."

Quarries

Bill Taylor continues: "A lot of the stone used in the buildings came from local quarries which were mainly freestone. The old Possil quarries stretched on both sides of what is now Balmore Rd in Lambhill near the police station and across the way to High Possil. The remnants of the old Lambhill Woods were still in evidence in the late 1940s as were the remains of two old water-filled quarries, the Pudge and the Ashes, where local boys used to sail rafts and collect frog spawn and baggies. Other quarries stretched from Kenmure and Colston to Bishopbriggs. There was a type of stone at Black Quarry Rockvilla which turned black when exposed to the air. Stone from Possil and Woodside was used in the construction of Hutchison's Hospital in Ingram St in 1802.

"Alec Thorn, whose family were local contractors from Lambhill, remembered sitting on the trams of the carts as the stone was brought down from the quarries at Kenmure and Colston for building work in Lambhill and Possil at the turn of the century. At the far end of Bardowie St, with parks stretching behind and along Lambhill Rd, was Keppoch Farm. This previously had been Harvey's Farm but before the turn of the century it was taken over by a man called Flanagan who let out his parks for football at a shilling a time. He had a boarhound dog and hadn't a great reputation for hard work. Possilpark has every reason to be proud of its history and shouldn't let anyone forget it."

Bill Taylor is the author of Glasgow North West*, a historical gem first published in 1976 which is still much sought after.*

Possil Characters

Saracen St has remained almost unchanged in spite of all the changes in many districts and has always been a meeting place for friends and neighbours over a long number of years. Possil produced many memorable characters such as Charlie McCann. This rotund bloke was liked by everyone. Charlie was a man of many talents. One of the clergy asked Charlie to act as MC at a 'hiv'tae' wedding in a single end at an address just off Garscube Rd. After the substantial 'kerryoot' arrived, the reception started with the five-piece band in the bed recess giving it belters. When the guests were well fortified Charlie decided to make an all important announcement: "Ladies and gentlemen you are all invited to the christening in the morning."

He was known for his Chic Murray take off and general good humour. He and his side-kick Tommy McKinnell were inseparable. Another popular figure was the red-headed Jimmy Gallagher, nicknamed Curly. Jimmy was liked by all he came in contact with and was just as well known on the island of Majorca where he had settled in the sixties. Wee Johnny O'Donnell from Hawthorn St was a well-known individual. Full of fun, he always had the coffin nail (Woodbine) stuck in his mouth. When bank loans were introduced in 1959 he went into the bank to make enquiries. The manager asked him, "How much do you want?" Johnny said, "How much have you got?"

The list of personalities in and around Possil over a long period is endless. Tommy Finnegan was the young manager of Cochrane's in Saracen St and knew everyone. Jimmy McLaughlan worked in Curley's the grocers for about 30 years and had a cheery word for all he came in contact with. Big John McGovern cut a dashing figure in his Scout kilt. My brother Jim, Pat Higgins, Davy Howard and Eric McQueen were all qualified and keen football referees. Matt Kerins was an electrician in John Brown's shipyard at the start of the war. He was working in the bowels of a ship in a confined space and hung his waistcoat on a hook which contained his tea and sugar can, a train ticket and five woodbine. Matt was leaving the yard when he remembered the waistcoat but the ship was already on its way to the war zone. The ship returned for much needed repairs after a four-year stint and Matt retrieved the waistcoat, just as he had left it. When his dog died suddenly, Matt, heartbroken, decided to give it a decent burial. He wrapped the animal very carefully in brown paper and placed it in a cardboard box and caught the 22 tram out to Lambhill. The box was left in the luggage space under the stairs and he went upstairs for a smoke. At the terminus he discovered the dead dog had been stolen.

Tommy Kerins was a popular figure in Possil over many years, especially in the Blind Asylum where he was employed all his working life. He was a colourful personality, full of fun and a good storyteller.

Reggie McColl was a likeable man with plenty of patter. Stevie and Tommy McKay had cousins from Garscube Rd who thought that the McKays were toffs because they had a bathroom. There were the Hoeys, Willie Crossan, Michael McLuskey, Jerry and Margaret Scullion, Michael White, John Desport and all the folk from the badminton club. John Brown, who had a long association with youth football, was always and still is, a nice man. One of the teachers at a Possil primary sent a note to a mother complaining about her daughter coming to school unwashed. Next day, the irate mother confronted the teacher. "Ma lassie's here tae be telt no smelt. She's no a bloomin' daffodil."

Many Possil families have moved on, such as the Scanlans, the Elliotts, the Shannons, the Brannans, the Blacks from Balmore Square and the musical and talented McCabe family; the Savage family, whose daughter Margaret achieved fame as the versatile lead singer with the popular Black and White Minstrel TV show; Freddie and Billy Yule and the Quigley brothers; Chrissie Myers was a nice gentle wee soul who spent a lifetime in the Blind Asylum; Hugh McMillan, Roger and Jacky Finnigan; John McVey was a real nice, gentle bloke who was the manager of the factor's office. He was also a good drummer and one of nature's gentlemen. There were Jim Leslie and the Buchanan family, the

Priors, Tommy Scott, Harry Sweeney, and Charlie and Kathleen McKenna who are still resident in Possil. All these folk contributed to the Possil of yesteryear.

Present-day Possilpark

In recent times, some changes have taken place. The health centre at Allander St and Barloch St (which resembles a mini-hospital) has been operational since the mid-eighties. Bingo is big business at the Bass Leisure Group in Hawthorn St which can cater for 2,000 patrons on a nightly basis, offering large money prizes. Possil Point and the Adult Education Centre provide a much-needed service to the community but like all these agencies they are struggling to survive because of funding cutbacks. Possilpark is connected to all the surrounding areas each with their own characters and atmosphere and has easy access to city life.

ELSEWHERE

Glasgow Jiggin'

Rikki Fulton and Jack Milroy immortalised the patter and style of dancing in the fifties with their Francie and Josie routine. "Are you dancin?" "Are you askin? Well Ah'm dancing." Glasgow was dancing mad. There were dance halls everywhere, especially in the city centre. In fact, at the Charing Cross end of town, there was a good selection to choose from, all within walking distance. The Albert in Bath St was a well established and popular dance hall which appealed to the formal ballroom type, anxious to improve their skills and progress to the bronze, silver and gold level. The management expected the patrons to behave with decorum and dress accordingly. It was very respectable. St Andrew's Halls, situated behind the Mitchell Library, attracted huge crowds where you could dance in either of its two halls. It was destroyed by fire in the sixties. The Mitchell Theatre now stands on this site. The Berkeley always had a mature and steady clientele whose preference was orthodox dancing with no frills. They didn't seem to mind negotiating the mirrored poles which occupied a section of the dance area. Further on down Berkeley St was the old established Musicians Club. Entry was by membership only or by invitation. At the St George's Rd end of Charing Cross, countless steps led up to the West End Ballroom. An older type of dancer graced these premises with their prowess. When some

The Locarno

of the incumbents got a bit fortified it added a couple of feet to their normal stature, and a different form of entertainment was instantly produced.

Around the corner into Sauchiehall St was the Astoria dance hall which was similar to the West End and attracted the old-fashioned punters. It could be a wee bit tense at times when the Yanks were in town.

The Locarno, also in Sauchiehall St, was one of the most up-to-date and popular dance halls in the city. Its plush decor and

'Come Dancing' competition, The Locarno

comfortable surroundings with the unique revolving band stage, made this venue a pleasure to dance in. Nat Allan was the resident band. Ray Ellington would be the guest group from time to time with his own particular brand of music.

Opposite the Pavilion Theatre in Renfield St was Green's Playhouse, a massive building which included a cinema at ground level with its 'golden divans' for courting couples. Dancing was in the upper floor of the building. All the big, popular dance bands appeared at the Playhouse. Syd Phillips was a memorable jazz band who made repeated appearances and the effervescent Joe Loss with Michael Holiday as the lead singer attracted large numbers. Couples would stop dancing and gather in front of the band to listen to Michael's Bing Crosby style of singing. Doctor Crock and his Crackpots were terrific. His band had a big, booming sound which could be heard all over Cowcaddens and the cabaret antics were highly entertaining. A short walk up Hillfoot St from Duke St in the east end was the Dennistoun Palais. All the regular dancing was advertised in the Evening Times: "The Palais De Dance Dennistoun. Dancing every evening 7.30 till 10.45 – -2/ – Laurie Blandford, Glasgow's leading band." Real fancy don't you think?

Both the Locarno and the Palais had girls whose preference was to dance with their pals. It did seem a bit odd at the time. They were usually dressed in a white blouse and dark skirt, talking ten to the dozen, chewing gum while doing the hesitation shuffle. It took a brave bloke to interrupt these Siamese twins who would give you the silent stare. The six-inch purse, full of all those big pennies and half crowns, clutched tightly in their palm, was a secret weapon. It could be dropped on your toes and make you a candidate for the Western Infirmary.

Barrowland in the Calton had a great atmosphere. It was always busy and had a good dance floor. Billy McGregor and the Gaybirds band (not politically correct in today's world!) were marvellous. They played all the popular music of the day. On the occasion when trouble interrupted the proceedings, the band just ignored the unwanted distraction and played louder. Barrowland jivers were legendary and competed vigorously to be recognised as the best. Teddy Boy knee-length jackets and drainpipe trousers were always evident in Barrowland. Jivers were a treat to watch because of their skill. Spaces would be made available to allow them to exhibit their impromptu routines.

At Eglington Toll, the ever-popular Plaza with its water fountain, was the longest surviving dance hall, which was still operating in the nineties, and catered for the enthusiastic ballroom dancers. A good number of the punters fancied their barra at the tango. There must be a lot of folk around Glasgow with sore backs when you consider the antics of those tango dancers.

Dancin' On

Many people preferred their local dance halls or parochial dancing in church halls. St Joseph's on Saturday nights was a sellout and was monitored by the resident priest. One time, having rehearsed my Protestant pal for days on certain prayers, and after a lengthy wait in a big queue, we at last reached the customs point. Anything to declare? Catholic or Protestant? We had just been admitted when my pal said to the priest: "Thank you very much, sir." "Out! Out!" We were ushered into the street, determined to try some other time.

Possil people were spoiled for choice for dance halls, all within easy reach. There was The Lorne, of course, and the Springburn Public; the Oddfellows near the top of Hawthorn St and also dancing in the Maryhill Public Halls.

The Lorne dance hall, in the grounds of Ashfield stadium, attracted many keen dancers. It had a marvellous dance floor. Big Albert Romeo, a Cesar Romero type figure at the door, was ever vigilant regarding troublemakers. There were times when he had to contain some turbulent behaviour from some of the punters, but he could sort things out in a jiffy.

Putting on the Style

In the late forties, George Raft, the legendary film star, performed the opening ceremony of McConnells gents' outfitters shop at the top of Renfield St Dressed in a white raincoat and a gangster-type fedora pulled over his right eye, he attracted huge crowds. He was a great tango dancer in some of his old films. Billy Eckstine, Johnny Ray and Frankie Laine appeared at the Glasgow Empire dressed with the most modern up-to-date fashions from the States. Everyone wanted to emulate their dress style. Remember the wee plastic bones that fitted into the points of the shirt collar? Some blokes had the lot. DA haircut, a full drape suit, Billy Eckstine shirt, oxblood coloured crepe soled shoes and of course, the Robert Mitchum walk – the coat hanger still in the jacket and wee short steps in order to leave the entire outfit undisturbed. Almost like Frankenstein with a girdle! Dozens of these Mitchum look-a-likes paraded on either side of the dance floor in the Locarno.

Fusco's in Cambridge St was the busiest barbers in town. They specialised in the Tony Curtis and Perry Como style, and also the DA hairstyle. At that fashionable time, short-back-and-sides was not in great demand. For many of the people who frequented the jiggin, the memories linger on of the days when they thought that the Francie and Josie style and patter only belonged to them.

The Round Toll

This was a busy junction on Garscube Rd and the beginning of Possil Rd. The points policeman, dressed in his big white cape and standing on a wooden platform in the middle of the Toll, directed traffic for a period of 18 years with remarkable patience. During peak times, when the traffic came to a standstill, he stepped down from his perch and walked down St George's Rd for a wee smoke. Inevitably, when he returned, everything was back to normal. The Tower Ballroom had the most notorious reputation for toughness in the whole area. Situated at the Round Toll, the ballroom was on the top floor. On Friday and Saturday nights all the hard men settled their differences at the dancin. It was believed that some individuals were thrown out of the windows during those epic battles, probably a bit of an exaggeration. Oakbank Hospital was very convenient for The Tower.

Oakbank Hospital

Oakbank, situated at Baird's Brae, rendered wonderful service to all and sundry from the cradle to the grave. The walking wounded were treated with great patience. Everyone queued in orderly fashion, sliding along those familiar benches waiting for treatment.

Cinemas

The Magnet cinema, which was just a short distance from Oakbank hospital, had the same bench seats. You were itching to get in and scratching to get out! It was fourpence for the privilege and had its own distinctive smell, a wee bit like the subway. Most people at that time would have preferred the clinical smell of acriflavine or gentian violet which was applied to the skint knees and other wounds of many individuals. The visible colour blend was actually quite nice, one leg yellow and the other purple! Also on Baird's Brae was the Astoria picture hall which could seat 3000 people. It was sevenpence for the stalls and ninepence for the balcony. The whole programme seemed to continue with hardly a break. Nine times out of ten, after a long wait in the queue, you saw the end of the picture before the beginning, and you were only allowed to stay for the duration of the film. Therefore, if you arrived in the middle of the film, you had to leave at the middle of the next showing! If the film was a thriller or a weepy picture the whole hall would be silent and tense until some eejit would drop his candy balls and they would roll down the slope like thunder and hit the kick board at the front stalls with such a clatter. The ushers didn't have the full uniform, only a skippet cap and a torch but they were the full shilling all right. They were tough with the patrons. It never failed to amaze me that they could shine their torch on you with complete confidence and utter those fearful words. "You came in at it this bit." You sat there petrified! It was uncanny.

Corporation Baths

Many families didn't have a bathroom, therefore the alternative was the Woodside Public Baths, which was in the proximity of the Round Toll, and was something else. After paying the fee at the turnstile you collected a big rough towel, not unlike the tex-

Astoria picture house at Baird's Brae and Round Toll

ture of an army greatcoat, and the standard issue of carbolic green soap usually the size of a brick and just as hard. Now for the exciting bit! The large iron baths were situated in a long row with a small partition to protect your dignity. The gruff attendant, armed with the large 'master spanner' turned on the boiling water which cascaded into all nine or 10 baths like the Niagara Falls, with squeals of pain and protests from all the participants. Screams of "It's too hoat" were completely ignored. He administered the recommended Corporation temperatures with little provision for cold water. That baths attendant with the Desperate Dan spanner wielded unquestionable power. When the incumbents were overcome by the feelgood factor and at peace with the world, each cubical door was battered followed by a loud command: "Times up, there's a big queue waitin'."

Corporation Drapers

Glasgow Corporation provided free clothes to needy children from their store in Garnethill. This service was much appreciated by many parents who had plenty of clothing coupons but no money. The recipients arrived early in the morning for the rigout. Everything was standard issue. Combinations, a one-piece garment with the bunker-lid flap held by two buttons at the rear, was bonded on to the body and buttoned up to the neck. This unique underwear could work its way below your wee short trousers, which was to be avoided. The top hose socks and jersey were duly fitted followed by the jaggy jaiket and trousers which were guaranteed to inflict all possible injuries to sensitive parts of the body. The fabric was a mixture of barbed wire, jaggy nettles and sisal. Obviously made for long-lasting wear! What about the boots? These, I suppose, were meant to outlive the war. They had 12 steel studs and heel plates. A special way of walking had to be acquired, as if crossing a farmer's field of cowpies. After a while though, they were nae bother. Girls' clothes were of a gentler nature.

Driving a Glasgow Taxi

The taxi outing down to Troon is a well-established annual Glasgow event for disadvantaged children which arouses great enthusiasm and is a well-organised, carnival affair. Children are treated like royalty on this, their special day. The taxis are colourfully decorated and the competition is fierce amongst the drivers for the coveted best-dressed taxi prize. Shortly after the Second World War, Tubby McLaren, a Possil taxi owner, and two of his companions took some children from East Park Home in Maryhill for an outing to Saltcoats. This wee effort of goodwill proved highly successful and the first committee formed what became known as 'The Kiddies' Outing'. Billy McGregor, the popular leader of the resident Gaybirds band in the Barrowlands, agreed to join those founding members. He provided the music for the event on into the fifties. In fact, on his retirement from the music business, he entered the taxi trade. Davy McNellis, the first

Taxi outing – founding members

chairman, was also a colourful character. He was an enthusiastic member of the taxi trade and his cab was an exception to the rule, which was the only blue and black taxi in the city.

From humble beginnings back in 1945, the 'Kiddies' Outing' has gone from strength to strength due to the hard work, loyalty and dedication of many people of goodwill. Children are transported from various hospitals and institutions in and around the city, with their carers to Kelvingrove for the outing to Troon. One person who deserves a lot of the credit for the continued success of this well-organised event is Billy McLaren. Many people were recipients of his kind assistance. Quite often Billy would attend the licensing court to plead for individuals in trouble.

Billy McLaren died in 1994. He was a magistrate for many years. A huge congregation attended the service in Rockvilla Parish Church, Possilpark, and listened intently to the eulogy given by Michael Martin MP. Billy's influence reached out to many persons in the political scene.

Glasgow Life

In the early sixties, working the streets of Glasgow in a black Hackney cab was a fun job, especially in the day time, although night shift could be precarious at weekends. At that period, life was very different in the taxi trade. A Hackney branch of police officers implemented and controlled the city taxis, testing all vehicles to a high standard. To qualify for the job as a taxi driver, a written and oral test had to satisfy the police that the applicant had a good working knowledge of the housing schemes, numerous docks and all the features of Glasgow, city wide.

Fun at the Fair

Glasgow Fair was party time and taxis were in big demand with families travelling to Central Station en route to Rothesay and other destinations. It was a happy occasion with the children dressed in their Sunday-best and the mother all harassed, struggling with two big heavy suitcases and no man to assist. I thought at that time only people in the top flat of tenements went on holiday and travelled with the heaviest cases. On the return journey it was murder with the cases bulging and having to be pushed, shoved and hauled back up to the top landing. A black taxi could be used for a variety of removals, taking furniture, linoleum, carpets, building material and flittings from bedsits from which you were expected to take everything but the kitchen sink.

Driving a cab can be a very lonely and high-risk occupation at times, but the characters in the taxi trade compensate, and help can be summoned at short notice. Due to advanced technology the driver has more protection, but working the streets improves the skills of observation and you learn to anticipate situations. It always amazed me when a couple were having a rammy. He would be giving his wife dog's abuse and then would address the driver in a very civil voice, "How is it goin' Jimmy, where are you goin' yer holidays?" Then the poor woman would be subjected to more threatening behaviour.

Before the leisure revolution changed city nightlife, public transport came to a halt at 11pm. Alternatively, people in the city had to walk to George Square for the all-night bus or take a taxi which was inexpensive. Many of the operators and drivers were known by their nicknames. Chippy Tarn, Coffee Joe, Man-in-a-suitcase, Big Cass, The Bull, The Fat Controller, The Budgie, The Mouse, Flying Officer, Sinbad, Big Sooty, Harry the Horse, Man Friday and the infallible Radio Controller referred to as 'God'.

Life and Death

The 'flying squad' was a job from Yorkhill Hospital to attend a home confinement. A doctor and nurse would wait anxiously to be picked up holding a big, black box containing the blood. On one occasion, the destination was a Maryhill tenement. When we arrived at the destination I told them to go ahead and I would follow quickly with the blood. Seconds later, they came running back in a panic. I asked what was wrong. "Driver, there's a fierce Alsatian at the door!" "Follow me," I instructed them. Brushing past the dog into the room, I saw the expecting mother lying on a couch giving birth, while another woman was screaming in utter panic. Putting the latter and the Alsatian into the bathroom, I returned to the taxi.

There were many scary times. I was first taxi at Anderston bus station when a young man calmly asked me to drive him to the nearest hospital. He had blood all over his right hand. Driving up Cathedral St towards the Royal Infirmary like a mad man, I noticed the cardigan he had been holding fall to the floor to reveal a large knife embedded in his stomach. He was sliding further down the seat as I told him not to move. A doctor and nurse treated him in the taxi for 10 minutes. He insisted on paying the fare plus a tip.

One of the well-known drivers became ill with cancer and had only six months to live. When news of his death was broadcast on the taxi radio a good number of his pals attended the service. To their dismay, when the celebrant spoke about the deceased's background and after a quick glance at the congregation, they realised they were at the wrong funeral! Naturally they all adjourned to the Arlington pub where many a soiree had been enjoyed with the deceased. The assembled company were in a state of shock when the alleged deceased entered the pub. "We've just been to your funeral!" It was discovered a short time later that it was, in fact, a taxi driver with the same name who had been in similar circumstances.

Unusual Hire

Gus Hoey, a well-known character in the taxi trade, was the first driver in the unofficial rank at the Broomielaw waiting for the 6.30am arrival of the cattle boat from Ireland. The first passenger came down the gang plank leading a young pony and asked directions to Central Station. "Jump on the pony's back and turn first left at Oswald Street and you will be there in a jiffy." The Irishman pleaded, "I've never been in Glasgow before and I am desperate to get to Ayrshire." Gus remonstrated. "You can't miss it, it's only two minutes from here." At this juncture, the Irishman produced a fiver and quick as a flash Gus said, "Get in!" The pony was reversed into the cab and the passenger door window was opened to allow the animal's head to protrude. Gus later remarked, "It was neigh bother".

One day, after the usual early-morning rush, I joined my taxi colleagues at the verandah rank at Central Station in good time for the arrival of the Ayrshire coastal trains. A fur-coated lady wearing a fancy hat poked her head in the window and in a convoluted accent commanded: "Pettigrew and Stephen's draiver." All the drivers knew the drill. This passenger expected the door to be held open at the beginning and termination of the hire. Hope St traffic wasn't a one-way system in those days, therefore it took ages to negotiate. Keeping her gaze firmly on the meter, she inquired, "Could you stop the meter at the traffic lights, draiver?" To keep the sowl happy you made a pretence of doing just that. As the fare was two and fourpence, she placed a warm half crown in your hand, which she probably had been holding since Lochwinnoch. "Keep the change, draiver." I remember one old wag remarking when he had the same hire and the same payment: "Thank you madame, ah'll weigh masel twice!"

Bowler Hats

At the verandah taxi rank, outside Central Station, a long waiting spell was an opportunity to clean the windows and polish the cab as the Hackney police surveyed the taxi ranks from time to time. They were fair but didn't hesitate to make reprimands regarding personal conduct and condition of the vehicle. In those far off days many business men and white-collar workers in the city carried a rolled-up umbrella and wore a black bowler hat placed squarely on the head, probably as a symbol of success and respectability. Walking along Gordon St, many of these gentlemen would raise their black hats and give us a friendly nod. In fact, management staff in the shipyards sported the same headgear as a sign of authority and it was believed the bowler was reinforced as protection from hot rivets. One particular bloke, immaculately dressed in his brown suit and proudly wearing a brown bowler hat at a jaunty angle, was a sight to behold. He gave the taxi drivers his customary nod, and would be pleased as punch when one or two of us would comment on his elegant appearance. He was referred to as Mr. Brown.

Landing on the Moon

One sunny, quiet Saturday morning the controller asked me to pick up a hire from a city pub. To my surprise, the hire was the one-and-only Mr. Brown who was leaning slightly towards Gourock. "Driver," he announced, "We are going to Langholm, after I drop my golf clubs at the house. You must also meet my wife." After promising his lovely, invalid wife I would take care of him and thinking, 'the rich can be really very poor', we set off on our journey. "Point the car at Edinburgh. We are going to visit Neil Armstrong, the American astronaut, who is receiving the freedom of Langholm." Approaching the capital city, my now sobering companion shouted, "Stop here driver, I can hear the sound of bagpipes!" He went AWOL for 20 minutes and returned with a walking stick, a half-bottle of Bell's whisky and two paper cups. We eventually reached Langholm at three in the afternoon to be told by the local policeman that the celebrations were over and Armstrong was ensconced in a castle somewhere in the far-off hinterland. My passenger was feeling no pain having scoffed his whisky. "We will go there, driver," he declared.

"It is time to return home," says I. "I've got tickets for the Clancy Brothers performing at the Odeon tonight." During the return journey my agreeable companion decided to make an antique safari at the border towns. After serious deliberations, a hunting horn was purchased from which I could produce a clear sound compared to his barely audible squeak. At our next stop on the safari he performed the same ritual viewing. All items were diligently examined, punctuated by many questions and my considered opinion. Possibly Mr. Brown judged me an expert because I was the proud owner of an antique 'C' reggi taxi. We emerged from the shop with a six-foot suit of armour. The locals were mesmerised at my efforts to place this object into the back of a Glasgow taxi. Eventually we arrived back in the city at 8.30pm, both of us shattered, and Mr. Brown commanded, "Stop here driver at my business premises and open the store. Would you kindly put my purchases inside the main door and carefully lock up. Take me home and call in on Monday morning for payment. It's been an interesting day!"

Render unto Caesar

In the spring of 1986 I was summoned to that dreaded address of the Inland Revenue in Waterloo St, Glasgow. The accounts were in order but my accountant and I were in dispute with Her Majesty's tax inspector regarding the average taxi fare. Over the long years in the taxi trade it was common knowledge that many people received harsh treatment when they were caught in the clutches of the taxman. Although my accountant and I had a healthy working relationship over a long period, he was a little apprehensive due to an embarrassing situation he had suffered with a client in the past, when the taxi driver's behaviour left him no alternative but to leave the client to settle his problems on his own. We were ushered into Waterloo St premises by two government representatives, both of us feeling a wee bit tense. The meeting commenced with general questions regarding my situation as a taxi proprietor and my considered opinion of the average fare working the streets of Glasgow. While the senior member was asking various questions his partner was silently taking copious notes. In fact, he continued to do so throughout the entire meeting. After approximately an hour and a half, the well-mannered gentleman asking the taxing questions pushed back his chair and invited me to talk about the taxi trade in general. With some years of experience in the trade I confidently launched into some aspects about the difficulties operating in the present financial climate as a taxi owner. How it affected family life and how individuals emerging from factories and shipyards would erect makeshift taxi signs on their private cars for weekend work. As public transport ceased to exist in the city after 11pm, the city fathers were only too willing to increase the number of taxis plying for hire. After talking non-stop for half an hour, my concluding remarks were about escalating costs and the three-year absence of a meter rise. The interrogation then continued with regard to private mileage. Realising that I had omitted to include extra journeys outside the city boundary to play football, I offered my apologies and was prepared to accept the consequences. All proceedings came to a halt. "You play football?" he asked. "I'm Tommy Walker. I played for Hearts." The whole atmosphere changed, becoming relaxed and friendly. We talked football and exchanged football anecdotes for almost 40 minutes while my accountant sat in flabbergasted silence at the turn of events. The tax inspector finally asked: "Where were we?" Our meeting in Waterloo St came to a close eventually and all concerned parted amicably. On leaving the building I invited my dumbstruck accountant to discuss our experience over a cup of coffee which he refused with these words: "You certainly know the taxi business. I'm going back to the office to hold a meeting with all the partners and persuade them to appoint you as the public relations officer." Glasgow people are the greatest, both in their generosity and cheery outlook and if you are considerate and helpful, taxi driving is a doddle.

Ruchill to Gweedore

At the beginning of March 1988, I received the news that my brother-in-law had died in America. He had lived in the States for 25 years although he was born and bred in Glasgow. His parents had moved from the west of Ireland to the Anderston district of Glasgow at the turn of the century and eventually raised their family in the densely populated district of Ruchill in the north of the city. During his lifetime he made frequent visits back to Ireland and took a keen interest in developments across the political spectrum; he was saddened by the tragic events which have resulted in much suffering and needless loss of life these past 20 years in that beleaguered country. Therefore, it was no surprise that the burial would take place in Gweedore, Donegal. His remains were flown to Belfast on that tragic day, Friday, March 11, 1988, when two soldiers in civilian clothes were brutally trapped in a cul-de-sac and killed by an angry mob.

At the funeral the next day, I was to discover that as a result of the tragedy the cortege had endured hours of delay in Belfast, as they waited for clearance from the authorities before permission was granted to proceed with the journey to Donegal. The cortege finally arrived in Derrybeg, Gweedore just before midnight. It had been 35 years since my last visit to that particular part of Ireland, which was a nightmare of a journey in those early days where passengers boarded the ferry at Broomielaw for the arduous crossing. The cheapest crossing was by steerage or third class, in other words no accommodation was provided. Night travellers had to sleep on the floor for the 12-hour crossing to Belfast, then endure the long journey north.

Travelling from the west end of Glasgow, I boarded the 1pm Loganair flight from Glasgow Airport arriving in Belfast at 2.15pm. Being the last passenger to disembark, with no knowledge of the city, I asked the pleasant stewardess for directions to the bus station. To my astonishment, she kindly offered to drive me there as her car was parked at the airport. This was a welcome start to the journey north because the rain was coming down in buckets. After making some enquiries, the alternative train link to Londonderry became more attractive. The train was jam-packed with students from Belfast University going home to Derry for the weekend. I spoke to a nice lad sitting opposite and explained my predicament. To my amazement, he informed me that Derry was the end of the line but his father was meeting him at the station and he would drive me to the bus terminus, which I was glad to accept. Thanking them for their assistance, I entered the Ulster bus station at 6.15pm to be told that the last bus had gone at 6pm and the bus station was closing until Monday morning. The requiem was due to take place at 10am the following morning and it was now 6.30pm on Friday evening. I was beginning to panic as my destination was still a long way off. The nice, sympathetic gentleman in the bus station suggested that he would drop me at the border location on the direct route to Letterkenny, which is 30 miles from Gweedore.

At the border, the soldiers were checking all the cars and refused to assist. It was understandable after the tragic events earlier in the day. Dressed in a light Burberry, with a small bag on my shoulder, I suppose in hindsight I may have been viewed as a suspicious figure. There was no alternative, hitching a lift was the only option open to me. By this time it was 7pm on a dark and drizzly Friday evening, miles from nowhere. Feeling weary and dispirited, I prayed fervently for help as I approached a large roundabout. There was an eerie silence about the area with very few cars on the road. After a considerable time waiting at the roundabout a small sports car stopped and a lovely Irish voice said: "I'm going as far as Letterkenny." This charming gentleman, a doctor, proved an interesting companion with a good knowledge of mainland Britain. Wishing to express my gratitude in some way, he rejected all my suggestions with his unforgettable parting remark, "Pass it on".

In the spare ground bus station, I made some enquiries about transportation to Gweedore. It was now 10.15pm. A helpful driver said that a bus was due in Letterkenny at 10.30pm from Galway and would be dropping passengers as far as Gweedore which was approximately an hour's journey. I was elated. The day's trauma was almost over. The long established Gallaher's Hotel was still in business in Derrybeg and the driver agreed to drop me at the door. After securing accommodation and telling the proprietor that I had come for the funeral, she was able to fill me in with all the details. News travels fast in Ireland. The only telephone available was in the public bar which was bedlam with shouting and singing. Of course, it was a quarter to 12 on a Friday night and the patrons were feeling no pain. Attempting to phone my wife in Glasgow by trying to feed the antiquated 'press button A and B' telephone was an impossible task. All I heard amidst the din was the operator in his parish priest Irish voice: "I have your good man safely here in Donegal." Then the line went dead. However, the next morning I felt refreshed and delighted that I had survived the previous day's events. I recalled the kindness I had encountered since my departure from Glasgow and I now had the time to view all the expected changes that had taken place since that first visit in 1952.

The first major change was that the old church had been replaced with a new modern one nearby and the wee shop opposite was now a spacious supermarket. Close to the top of the hill before the shore road was the popular and comfortable Errigal Hotel, usually filled with American visitors. McNellis's Lodge at the top of the hill hadn't changed at all! After the moving funeral service, the remains were conveyed to the old shore cemetery in dignified silence.

Grief is a difficult burden to cope with but we realise that death is a celebration of a life. Before his departure to Canada and eventually into the United States my brother-in-law had been the popular manager of Saxone's shoe shop in Argyle St for a number of years. Like so many people from Glasgow in the fifties, the common practice was for the husband to cross the Atlantic on his own and after securing work and accommodation, the family would be united in their adopted country. Sadly, often a bereavement is the only opportunity for family relations and friends to get together. How many times have we remarked, "It's sad that families only come together in these circumstances".

During the regular Sunday midday service which was celebrated in both Gaelic and English, there was a predominance of young families present, probably due to new industries established in Gweedore which obviously created an atmosphere of confidence and prosperity in the area. Many of the bereaved had made the entire journey from the south of England with their own transport and it was a great relief when the deceased's brother agreed to drive me to the Belfast harbour airport for my 6pm flight back to Glasgow. He was booked for the Larne ferry crossing at 7.15pm and mentioned that he had a spare ticket if required.

After innumerable cups of tea, constant blethering and anxiously checking the time, we eventually left Gweedore in his powerful Jaguar car. Approaching the route to the airport, there were burnt-out buses and lorries dumped at the side of the road, evidence of the destruction and violence which was seen frequently on television. My Good Samaritan driver, unfamiliar with the city as I was, and anxious to deliver me on time, was mistakenly travelling towards the international airport. After some enquiries, we found the cluster of huts which make up the Harbour airport. He then took off like a bat out of hell for the Larne ferry, as it was the last crossing that evening.

My troubles weren't over yet. I had missed my connection by five minutes and the airport was closing until the next day. I was a lone figure standing in the rain at the entrance feeling dejected and despairing when, suddenly, a taxi appeared from nowhere. The driver couldn't guarantee that we would reach the ferry on time as road conditions were deplorable but we did, indeed, arrive at the large terminal with five minutes to spare. The security staff accepted my explanation regarding the available spare ferry ticket and ushered me on to the electric bus which slowly conveyed passengers from the terminal building to the ferry gangway. My friend in his Jaguar was situated at the head of the queue awaiting the signal to drive on to the ferry when I jumped from the bus and sprinted towards his car. He was absolutely shocked at seeing me. Regaining his composure and with a quizzical look, he said: "Did you drop in by parachute?" We made our way to the restaurant and were joined by some of the funeral party, most of whom were returning to England but three others were bound for Glasgow. All of them had missed the afternoon crossing.

Disaster seemed to touch us all on this ill-fated weekend but we were all feeling buoyant that we were nearing our journey's end. During a conversation with the deceased's sister about my weekend adventure, her concluding words were: "I want the name of that saint you pray to!"

More surprises were in store for the Glasgow party when it was realised that the ferry would miss the last train connection from Stranraer to Glasgow. My wife would be extremely worried to discover that I wasn't on the plane at Glasgow. It was imperative that contact was made as soon as possible. This modern ferry must have a phone! The purser directed me to the navigation deck where I was told that there was a landline, but the call would be three pound fifty pence. Hearing my wife as clear as a bell, she gasped in disbelief when I said I was calling from the middle of the Irish Sea and in the background my brother-in-law asked: "Is he walking it?" Fortunately, the Glasgow contingent was collected at Stranraer and arrived home safely in the wee small hours. An Irish odyssey of disasters!

A Visitor From Outer Space - The High Possil Meteorite

The High Possil meteorite fell on the morning of Thursday, April 5, 1804 in a quarry near High Possil, on the northern outskirts of Glasgow. The High Possil meteorite is one of only three ever to have been found in Scotland, the others being the Perth meteorite of 1830, and the Strathmore meteorite, which fell in Perthshire in 1917. Although meteorite falls are rare everywhere, Scotland seems to have escaped unexpectedly lightly from such bombardment. Over 18 falls are known in England and Wales. This effect may be more apparent than real, as much of Scotland is only sparsely populated, and the results of any unseen falls would rapidly become untraceable in the extensive tracts of mountain, bog, loch and forest. The High Possil is a stony meteorite, classified as an L6 hypersthene chondrite, a very common type. The Hunterian specimen, GLAHMM172, now weighs about 151g, and is the largest surviving piece of the meteorite. Although extra terrestrial in origin, the High Possil meteorite is mostly made up of minerals which also occur on earth. The major constituents are similar to those of a basalt: orthopyroxene, olivine, plagioclase feldspar and diopside. About nine per cent of the meteorite consists of nickel iron alloys, with traces of other metallic minerals such as troilite, merrillite, chromite and copper.

This text is by John Faithfull and is largely based on work by Graham Durant.

Possil meteorite

THE HIGH POSSIL METEORITE

From the *Herald and Advertiser*, Monday April 30th, 1804

We have been favoured with the following circumstantial account of a phenomenon in the neighbourhood which is at present the subject of much conversation and philosophical enquiry. "Three men working in a field in Possil, about three miles north from Glasgow, in the forenoon of Thursday the 5th curt, were alarmed with a singular noise, which continued, they say, for about two minutes, seeming to proceed from the south east to the north west. At first, it appeared to resemble four reports from the firing of cannon, afterwards, the sound of a bell, or rather of a gong, with a violently whizzing, and lastly they heard a sound, as if some hard body struck, with very great force the surface of the earth.

"On the same day, in the forenoon, six men were at work in the Possil quarry 30 feet below the surface of the ground, and there too an uncommon noise was heard, which, it is said, seemed at first to proceed from the firing of some cannon; but afterwards, the sound of hard substances hurling downwards over stones, and continuing in whole, for the space of a minute.

"By others who were at the quarry, viz. the overseer at the quarry and a man upon a tree, to whom he was giving directions, the noise is described as continued about two minutes; appearing as if it began in the west, and passed around by the north towards the east ... as if three or four cannons had been fired off about the bridge which conducts the Forth and Clyde over the River Kelvin, at the distance of a mile and a half westward from the quarry; and afterwards, as a violent rushing whizzing noise. Along with these last people, there were two boys, one often, and the other of four years old, and a dog; who on hearing the noise, ran home, seemingly in a great fright. The overseer, during continuance of the noise, on looking up to the atmosphere, observed in it a misty commotion, which occasioned in him a considerable alarm, when he called out to the man in the tree, 'Come down, I think there is some judgement coming upon us', and says that the man on the tree had scarcely got up on the ground, when something struck with great force, in a drain made for turning off water in the time of, or after rain, about ninety yards distance, splashing mud for about twenty feet around.

"The elder boy, led by the noise to look up to the atmosphere, says that he observed the appearance of smoke in it, with something reddish colour moving rapidly through the air, from the west till it fell on the ground. The younger boy, at the instant before the smoke against the earth was heard, called out 'Oh such a reek!' and says that he saw an appearance of smoke near the place where the body fell on the ground. The overseer immediately ran up to the place where the splashing was observed, where he saw a hole made at the bottom of the drain. In that place a small stream of water perhaps about a quarter of an inch deep, was running over a gentle declivity, and no spring is near it. The hole was filling with water, and about six inches of it remained still empty. The overseer having made bare his arm, thrust his hand and arm into the hole which he judges to have been almost perpendicular, the bottom being perhaps rather a very little inclined to the east and the upper part to the west; at the bottom of the hole he felt something hard, which he could not move with his hand. The hole was then cleared out, with a shovel and mattock, from an expectation that a cannon ball might be found, but nothing was observed except the natural stratum of soil, and a soft sandy rock upon which it lay, and two pieces of stone that had penetrated a few inches through the rock. The pieces of stone, he took to be whinstone, and thinks that they were eighteen inches below the bottom of the drain and thinks the hole was about fifteen inches in diameter. He was not sensible of any particular heat in the water or in the pieces of stone, nor of any uncommon smell in the latter, although he applied them to his nostrils. He says that the one piece was about two inches long; that the other piece was about six inches long, four inches broad, and four inches thick, blunted at the edges and end; that the fractures of pieces exactly coincided; that he does not know whether the fracture was caused by the violence of the fall, or by the mattock; and that he never saw any such stone about the quarry.

"Some days later, when the particulars which have been narrated became known, a careful search was made for these pieces of stone, which had been disregarded, and the first mentioned piece was soon found; but the largest piece having been used as a block in the quarry, and having fallen among rubbish, could not be discovered. Some days later, a fragment of it was detected. The two fragments recovered make the two extremes of the stone; on the surface, they are pretty smooth, and of a black colour but internally they have a greyish appearance. The intermediate part larger than both seems, as yet, to be lost.

"At the village of High Possil which is within a quarter of a mile of the place where the stone fell, the noise gave much alarm to those who were in the open air; and there seems, they thought that the sound proceeded from south east to north west, agreeably to the report of the three men first mentioned.

"Two men at work within a hundred yards of the house of Possil were alarmed by the noise; they thought it over their heads, and that it resembled the report of a cannon six times repeated at equal intervals, with a confused uncommon sound of ten minutes duration; the noise seemed to begin in the north, and to turn round by the west, south and east, to the north.

"The 5th. curt. was cold and cloudy; a little more cloudy to the north east than in the other quarters.

"It would gratify many who have heard the above circumstances, to learn, through the Glasgow Newspapers, whether any remarkable noise was observed in the neighbouring parts of the country on the forenoon of the 5th curt. that had any resemblance to what was remarked near Possil."

April 30th 1804

Footnote

On Saturday April 3, 2004, a plaque was unveiled by John Faithfull in Possilpark Library to mark the 200th anniversary of the Possil meteorite followed by a talk and presentation.

Postscript

A special event took place on an overcast Friday morning, May 20, 2005. The commemorative stone located at the north-east bend of the Possil Marsh walkway was in place. The opening ceremony was performed by Glasgow City councillor Helen Hurcombe who spoke about the early formation of the working party, expressing gratitude for the contribution made by Alex McNeill from Land Services [Parks Development]. He worked tirelessly behind the scenes to make the project a success.

Professor John Faithfull from the Hunterian Museum summarised the history of meteorites in Scotland. He also spoke about the dramatic effect the Possil Meteorite had on the local population at that time. Those in attendance included former members of Lambhill Community Council, the meteorite working party, Scottish Wildlife Trust, local people and a representative from Glasgow Public Libraries. Fr Noel Burke, who spent almost 12 years of his ministry in Lambhill and retains a keen interest in the area, was also present.

Meteorite Committee

Metro Vicks – All Stars and All Ages

Possil Young Team

Rows of men

St Agnes' drama club

The Alexander family

Washhouse women

Terry Welsh Obituary from *The Herald*, June 29, 2006

TERRY WELSH, a popular local historian and author, has died, aged 74. Although well-known in the west end of Glasgow, Terry's charitable work and writings on pre-war and post-war Glasgow established his name in the city and beyond.

Terry grew up in the mining community of Lambhill and his formative years gave him material for his compelling book, *Reflections: Lambhill, Possil and Elsewhere*, in which he committed the oral history of the time to print.

His writings on the Cadder Pit disaster, which claimed 11 lives on August 3, 1913, provide a vital historical record, as does his recording of the immigrant and native families who formed those communities.

As a 16-year-old surface worker at Balmore coal mine, he was no stranger to the harshness of mining life, but was never slow to reflect on the communal spirit that permeated industrial Glasgow society. Life was hard, but moments of epiphany were to be found.

He wrote: "Lambhill was a big adventure playground, with open country bordered by the canal and lush farmland ... it was a wonderful sight to watch the majestic Gypsy Queen pleasure boat glittering white in the sunlight, sailing west from Mavis Valley mining village, moving calmly beyond the mountain of pit-bing and heap of discarded waste, a reminder of hard sweat and toil of generations of miners."

The Second World War and the changing face of society are reflected in the Lambhill characters and landmarks, such as the Blind Asylum, on Saracen Street, then the world's largest industrial workshop for the visually impaired. It was also in Lambhill where he met and married his wife, Mary Kerins.

Terry led a rich and varied life. He worked as a shopkeeper in Lambhill, where he owned the general store in Balmore Road between 1975 and 1981. After three years in Canada, where he was employed as a welder, he returned to Glasgow and worked as a taxi proprietor until his retirement.

He was involved in Christian and volunteer work throughout his life, beginning at an early age with membership of the Young Christian Workers (YCW). He then became a member of the St Vincent de Paul (SVDP) Society, which he represented on the archdiocesan council.

Through the SVDP, he became involved in prison visiting and was a member of Hope, an organisation set up to aid prisoners and their families. Through the SVDP, he provided assistance for the Scottish Churches Housing Association, a charity that helped homeless people to be rehoused.

"He was one of the very few people who, if you asked him to go a mile for you, he would go two," reflected Father Willie Slaven, of St Simon's Church in Partick, and a close friend.

The Western Baths club in the west end of Glasgow, where he attended circuit training and played five-a-side football into his seventies, provided him with another outlet for his outgoing nature. He was a paradox: an extrovert who wanted other people and their achievements to be the centre of attention.

Last year he was diagnosed with throat cancer and fought it with the positivity with which he approached everything else in his life. As a devout Christian, his final months were marked by a belief in the riches which awaited him in eternal life.

"Grief is a difficult burden to cope with, but we realise that death is a celebration of a life," he wrote in *Reflections*.

Anyone whose life was touched by Terry will appreciate the resonance of those words.

He is survived by his loving wife, Mary.

★ ★ ★

I wrote the above obituary on Terry – a close friend of my family's – for *The Herald* in June 2006. After his death, *Reflections* continued to attract an audience and his widow, Mary, would regularly dispatch copies to interested readers at home and abroad. However, with the sudden death of Mary – a vibrant, loving and generous woman – in 2009, the book could no longer reach new readers. Digital publishing offered a new avenue and, so ... here it is. All proceeds from the book will go to the MacMillan Cancer Support charity.

Martin Greig
June 2013